The 10 Best-Ever Anxiety Management Techniques

Techniques

Workbook

The 10 Best-Ever Anxiety Management Techniques

Workbook

Margaret Wehrenberg

W. W. Norton & Company
New York • London

Copyright © 2012 by Margaret Wehrenberg

Digital production by Joe Lops
Composition by Bytheway Publishing Services
Book design by Jonathan D. Lippincott
Manufacturing by Courier Westford
Production Manager: Leeann Graham

Library of Congress Cataloging-in-Publication Data
Wehrenberg, Margaret.
The 10 best-ever anxiety management techniques workbook / Margaret Wehrenberg.
       p. cm.
Includes index.
ISBN 978-0-393-70743-4 (pbk.)
1. Anxiety.   2. Anxiety—Treatment.   I. Title.   II. Title: Ten best-ever anxiety management
techniques workbook.
BF575.A6W443 2012
152.4'6—dc22
2011013828

W. W. Norton & Company, Inc., 500 Fifth Avenue, New York, N.Y. 10110
www.wwnorton.com
W. W. Norton & Company Ltd., Castle House, 75/76 Wells St., London W1T 3QT
1 2 3 4 5 6 7 8 9 0

To the clients who have educated me about anxiety,

with thanks for their persistence and courage.

Contents

PART IV: **MANAGING ANXIOUS BEHAVIOR**

Acknowledgments

Producing this workbook was in no small way due to the assistance and vision of my editor at W. W. Norton, Andrea Costella Dawson, and Casey Ruble, my much-more-than copyeditor. Both of you have given me encouragement, prodding, and suggestions in just the right amounts.

I am deeply appreciative of the clients I have worked with over the years, who tried ideas that blossomed into techniques that were refined with their work over time.

So many dear friends are mental-health professionals too, and our ranging conversations have supplied me with fuel for the work and encouragement to get it down on paper. Special thanks to the "Pittsburgh Consultation Group +1," Laurel Coppersmith, Sandra Faulkner, Nancy Hoffman, and Mary Jane Murphy. I also thank Shannon Burns, Susan Cherwien, Martha Strauss, Michele Wiener-Davis, Mary Lou Carney, and Lurlene McDaniel, all of whom have contributed to my knowledge and direction in ways they all know.

I remain grateful to my family for their loving support.

The 10 Best-Ever Anxiety Management Techniques

Workbook

Introduction

The idea for a companion workbook to *The 10 Best-Ever Anxiety Management Techniques* has been in the works for some time. Shortly after that book was published, it became clear that people were using the book as a means of identifying and addressing their own anxiety problems. I have received numerous messages of appreciation for the ideas in that book. Both therapists and individuals asked for a way to work through each of the ideas it presented, wanting a guide for completing the techniques and structuring their progress.

This workbook provides both structure and clarification on how to make the techniques work. Chapters coincide with those in *The 10 Best-Ever Anxiety Management Techniques*, with added charts, worksheets, and self-assessment tools that will help readers see the effects of their anxiety. The checklists and self-assessments are based on situations I have observed over the years in my practice. As such they are not validated tests but rather represent questions I ask my clients and the circumstances they describe to me.

These simple assessments are followed by several methods that will correct the type of anxiety you are experiencing. Some people will benefit from working through all the techniques whereas others will need only a few to master the anxiety in their lives.

An added component to the workbook is a CD with 10 methods that complement the 10 techniques. Readers will be able to practice methods of breathing, mindfulness, and relaxation with audio guidance as they listen.

I am well aware that many people have other serious mental-health conditions in addition to anxiety. My intent is not to solve every problem but rather to make it easier for readers to move forward in their progress with other conditions, freed from debilitating anxiety symptoms. If anxiety has originated in trauma or difficult experiences during early life, those conditions probably require more help than is available in this workbook. If your anxiety is severe or persistent, seek help from a psychotherapist. However, improving anxiety and increasing the certainty that you can manage anxiety symptoms makes other mental health concerns easier to deal with. It is my hope that readers who follow the techniques for managing their anxiety symptoms will experience a relief they never knew possible.

PART I

Assess Yourself

ONE

What Kind of Anxiety Do I Have?

Anxiety. Stress. Worry. Panic. These words get thrown around a lot in everyday language, and people use them to refer to a wide range of feelings and experiences. But in the clinical sense, these terms have specific definitions with critical differences.

Stress is one condition everyone knows: When challenges come our way we respond with physical and mental reactions that are aimed to tolerate and resolve the stress. Not all stress is bad: A certain amount can promote our growth. For instance, a challenging project at work might help you improve your organizational skills and expand your creativity. That kind of stress could be called "eustress"—as opposed to "distress," which is what most of us mean when we talk about stress. "Distress" is when we are faced with something too challenging or even overwhelming, causing us physical tension and mental anguish.

Anxiety can create stress or be a response to it. Anxiety is the experience every person has in response to ambiguity. When we are uncertain, we feel a certain sensation in our gut and our thoughts turn toward figuring it out. We begin "what if" thinking—"What if _____ happens? What if I _____?"—as a means to figure out the ambiguity and resolve anxiety.

"What if" thinking when we feel anxiety in the absence of an actual problem becomes *worry.* "What if my son doesn't adjust well to preschool?" "What if I can't handle the increased responsibilities my new job will demand?" Worry is the mental condition in which we are preoccupied with a problem, having repetitive and distressing thoughts that intensify sensations of anxiety.

Panic is a state of terror without a good reason for it: intense physical arousal and terrified thoughts of dying, going crazy, or losing control.

This book will help you better manage these troublesome states of mind. Let's now take a closer look at anxiety.

Anxiety is a very real medical issue with symptoms that are:

- Emotional (dread, fearing panic, fearing social situations, etc.)
- Physical (racing heart, dizziness, shortness of breath, lump in the throat, tingling, etc.)
- Mental (worrying, preoccupation with fear, fear of dying or going crazy, etc.)

There is a critical difference between panic and acute anxiety. Many people think they "panic all day," but in the clinical sense, a true panic attack is quite brief—only minutes in duration. That said, the aftermath of a panic attack can last for hours, leaving a person tired, weak, and nauseous, with a "gut feeling" that something is wrong. We'll look more closely at panic attacks in Part II.

Acute anxiety is an intense feeling of dread or doom, but it does not have the intense heart-pounding physical arousal that goes with panic. It is a sense of anticipation of trouble. You might have this sensation when you receive a phone call saying your child is injured at school, or if your parent goes to the hospital with chest pain, or if your spouse says, "We have to talk," with no indication of what that talk is about. In these situations, you feel intensely worried. Your heart rate rises a little, you feel a bit sick, and you can think of nothing but whether things will be okay. That heightened negative mental and physical arousal continues until you know things are okay or have a sense that you can do something to deal with the situation. This acutely anxious feeling can go on for hours.

Another important distinction to understand is the difference between *feelings* of panic or anxiety and anxiety *disorders*. Anyone can experience feelings of panic or anxiety, and the presence of such feelings doesn't necessarily mean you have an anxiety *disorder*. It is only when you become preoccupied with avoiding feelings of panic and anxiety—to the point that you begin changing your life—that you are considered to have an anxiety disorder.

There are several different kinds of anxiety disorders:

- Panic disorder
- Generalized anxiety disorder
- Social anxiety disorder
- Agoraphobia

- Specific phobia
- Post-traumatic stress disorder (PTSD)
- Obsessive-compulsive disorder (OCD)

We'll look at each of these more closely later in the chapter.

Different kinds of anxiety have different causes and worsen in common life situations. Some causes are:

- Genetic predisposition to feel anxiety when under stress
- Experiencing anxiety as extremely unpleasant and something that must be avoided at all costs
- Exceptional or ongoing stress
- Trauma in the recent or distant past
- Other diverse medical, biological, or life situations

Certain kinds of medical conditions can cause symptoms identical to those of anxiety, so before you assume you suffer from anxiety, you need to see a physician for a checkup to rule out these medical conditions. Also, many medications can create side effects of anxiety. Although it's uncommon, even medications your physician might prescribe to calm you down can have unintended effects of raising anxiety. Common medical-condition causes of anxiety-like symptoms include problems with:

> Hint: It's a good idea to get a medical exam to make sure no physical disease or condition is creating your anxiety sensations.

- Heart
- Thyroid
- Blood sugar (diabetes or hypoglycemia)
- Hormone changes
- Stimulating drugs, such as steroids or those prescribed for asthma
- Medication side effects or adverse reactions

Ironically, many people with anxiety consult their physician far too often when they do *not* have a medical condition causing their anxiety symptoms. The physical sensations of anxiety lead them to believe that their problems *must* be physical because they are felt in the body. Anxiety does have physical symptoms and implications, but it does not necessarily stem from a disease or medical condition.

It is no surprise that anxiety has different causes and comes in different forms. Some people suffer panic attacks that come out of the blue; other people feel consumed by worry on a nearly constant basis. It is also no surprise that some people have confusing combinations of anxiety symptoms. Some wonder if their anxiety is normal or might actually be a disorder. Especially when life events are anxiety-provoking, it can be hard to know if your anxiety is a normal reaction or has become a problem that needs attention.

Regardless of the origin of your symptoms, once you feel anxiety, you will benefit from the techniques in this workbook. The following sections will help you identify what kind of anxiety you suffer from.

PANIC DISORDER

Panic attacks are bouts of sudden, intense physical and emotional feelings of fear or terror that last for 11 to 13 minutes. They typically leave you feeling weak, exhausted, and scared for minutes or even hours after the attack subsides.

Have You Suffered a Panic Attack?

Check off your symptoms in the following list. During the attack, did you experience:

☐ Rapid heart rate
☐ Rapid, shallow breathing
☐ Nausea
☐ Sweating
☐ Urge to urinate or diarrhea
☐ Tightness or pain in your chest
☐ Feeling that you cannot breathe or cannot catch your breath
☐ A lump in your throat or choking sensation
☐ Shaking/trembling
☐ Dizziness
☐ Feelings of unreality
☐ Belief that you are dying, going crazy, or about to lose control

If you felt 5 or more of these symptoms, you probably suffered a panic attack.

It's possible to experience panic attacks without suffering from panic *disorder*. Panic attacks are unpleasant. They are inconvenient. You are not happy to have them. But in and of themselves, they are not a mental health disorder. It is rather *worrying about* having panic attacks and *changing your life* to avoid them that indicates panic disorder.

Do You Have Panic Disorder?

If you have experienced at least one panic attack, check which of the following changes you have made. Have you:

☐ Worried about having panic attacks so much that you were distracted from work or social exchanges

☐ Stopped attending activities you previously enjoyed

☐ Limited driving to roads on which you feel safe from panic

☐ Avoided transportation that you think you might panic on and not be able to leave at will (e.g., a subway, bus, plane, boat, ferry)

☐ Avoided social situations where you fear you might panic (e.g., parties, stadiums)

☐ Stayed out of theaters, restaurants, or public meeting places for fear you will panic

☐ Started paying attention to exits and ways to escape a location

☐ Gone to the emergency room more than once to make sure you were not having a heart attack

☐ Avoided going into classrooms with too few or too many other students

☐ Stayed home from school for fear of having an attack

☐ Stopped shopping in stores when there are people who might observe you panicking (e.g., started grocery shopping late at night)

☐ Stopped exercising because you feared that rapid heart rate or respiration would trigger a panic attack

☐ Insisted that a family member or friend accompany you for travel, even for short distances, or accompany you into retail stores

How many did you check? If you checked:

1 = You don't have panic disorder yet, but don't make this behavior a habit! Know that you can control panic better than you can control situations or people.

2 = You are starting to change your behavior to accommodate panic. Ask yourself if giving up activities or making life more complicated is *really* better than managing panic.

3 = You may have panic disorder. You are certainly afraid of feeling afraid! Although this does not guarantee that you have the disorder, you are definitely changing your life to avoid panic attacks.

4 or more = Avoiding panic is controlling your life. You will benefit from learning how to stop panic attacks and you may want some guidance to begin doing things you have been avoiding.

The problem with avoiding panic attacks is that it works. But by changing your life to avoid panic, you hand over your control to the panic.

AGORAPHOBIA

Some people develop agoraphobia (fear of public places) as a result of avoiding panic attacks. For them, the avoidance offers so much relief that the subsequent loss of social engagement seems inconsequential. Losing out on fun and time with others seems a small price to pay for not feeling afraid (panicking). Some people with agoraphobia are so limited that they rarely leave their homes, whereas others go out but severely curtail where they go and with whom (e.g., they will not cross a bridge or go into a stadium). Inability to escape is a major concern. The range of choices of where you can go and whom you can go with narrows until leaving the house requires thought, as shown in Figure 1.1.

This book does not address agoraphobia directly. If the agoraphobia started with panic, then managing panic successfully should help you undo the fear of going out. If your agoraphobia did not begin with panic, there are probably complicating factors that require psychotherapy.

GENERALIZED ANXIETY

Whereas those with panic disorder have a specific, single fear (fearing a panic attack), people with generalized anxiety disorder worry constantly about a wide variety of things. These things may change over time, but the condition of worry remains constant.

The serious impairment to life that generalized anxiety engenders is grossly underestimated. The gnawing feeling in your gut, the preoccupation and loss of attention, the sense of doom and misery, and the physical agitation all combine to create major impediments to participating in life. Loss of pleasure and constant worry undermine daytime activities as well as sleep, so that you have no respite even during the night.

You may wonder if your worry is severe enough to be considered a dis-

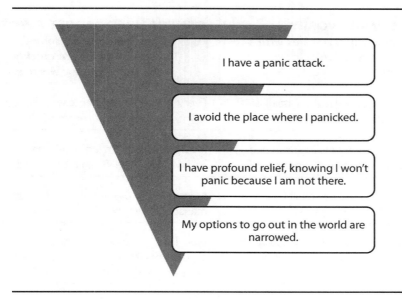

Figure 1.1 Agoraphobia Narrows Choices

order. Figure 1.2 lists the differences between "normal" worry and excessive worry.

Do You Have Generalized Anxiety?

If the items in the "excessive worry" column in Figure 1.2 seem to pertain to you, read the following list and check off the questions you can answer "yes" to.

☐ I worry a lot on most days and this has been going on for 6 months or more.

☐ I ruin whole days or good events by worrying, and my worries are often unreasonable, even though they are about normal things like work, school performance, physical health, or friendships.

☐ No matter how hard I try, I cannot seem to stop the worry.

If you answered "yes" to these three questions, your anxiety is greater than normal and you may have generalized anxiety disorder.

NORMAL WORRY Situation-specific, resolves with resolution of the situation	GENERALIZED ANXIETY WORRY Excessive time consumed, resolved worries are quickly replaced with new worries
I am worried about my daughter being safe on a mountain-climbing expedition.	Every time my daughter leaves the house, I worry that she won't return safely.
I worry about the safety of driving in bad weather, and am very cautious on the road.	I feel intensely worried about the weather and will not drive if rain is predicted.
I worry about how I will pay a bill that is unexpected, and I try to figure it out.	I worry every day about how I would manage financially if I lost my job.
When my kids have a physical symptom like a fever, I worry about whether it will get too high and I watch them carefully.	I feel frantic with worry whenever my children have a fever or other physical symptom and am afraid they will die.
I am worried before I take a test about how hard it will be and if I will get a passing grade.	I worry about not being smart enough and am constantly comparing my grades to those of my friends.
I worry about my spouse's drug relapse damaging our relationship permanently.	Whenever I am in a relationship I worry about when it will end.
I want my children to be safe, so I research whether chemicals I use around the house could be toxic if they are ingested.	I am constantly worried about whether my children will be harmed by environmental toxins and I am always online searching for hazards I may not be aware of.
I sometimes worry if I have an unusual physical symptom, and I check it out with a doctor if the symptom does not go away in a reasonable time.	I research all my symptoms online, no matter how minor they are, to be sure I don't have a serious disease.

Figure 1.2 Normal Worry Versus Excessive Worry

Certain physical conditions accompany generalized anxiety. They are the result of the underlying brain chemistry that creates worry, and of the worry it-self, which produces tension.

> ### Do You Have Physical Symptoms of Generalized Anxiety?
> Check the box below if you experience:
>
> ☐ Muscle tension, including TMJ (temporomandibular joint disorder) or neck/back ache
> ☐ Headaches
> ☐ Irritable bowel syndrome (aggravated by tension)
> ☐ Irritability
> ☐ Restless sleep or fatigue on awakening
> ☐ Physical jumpiness
>
> If you have three or more of these, pay careful attention to Technique #1 about changing your intake and Technique #4 on relaxation. And watch for the feelings of depression that follow prolonged worry and anxiety. There is a big overlap between depression and generalized anxiety, and once you become depressed, your energy to overcome the anxiety will be seriously depleted. You may need psychotherapy help to work on those disorders.

SOCIAL ANXIETY DISORDER

People who are shy know the symptoms of social anxiety in a mild way. You may not want to be the center of attention or perform in public. There is nothing wrong with being shy, and most shy people have satisfying lives without their shyness getting in the way of accomplishments. But when you have social anxiety, there are big impairments in fulfilling your potential because you avoid challenging experiences that could help you grow and develop your abilities. Social anxiety may be something you are born with, and it gets worse for most people who do not get good help. It can be seen in childhood, adolescence, or adulthood. Most people with social anxiety experience their anxiety as too uncomfortable to tolerate. They are sensitive to the very feeling of anxiety and try to avoid feeling it.

There are three categories of common symptoms for social anxiety, which involve avoiding whatever it is that might make you feel uncomfortable. These have to do with feeling uncomfortable being observed, anticipating being judged for inevitable social gaffes, or having mistaken beliefs.

Do You Have Social Anxiety?

What is your score in these three categories? The typical ways that people fear being observed are varied. Check statements that apply to you.

Do you fear being observed while:

☐ Eating in a restaurant
☐ Signing a check or credit-card receipt
☐ Answering a question at school
☐ Speaking up at a business meeting
☐ Leaving your seat during a movie or theater performance

People with social anxiety also fear being judged. Do you fear that in social situations you will:

☐ Not be able to think of interesting things to say
☐ Not be likeable
☐ Blush or be silent when meeting new people
☐ Reveal some social inadequacy, such as wearing the wrong clothes or not know a "social grace" such as which fork to use at a set table
☐ Embarrass yourself by saying the wrong thing

If you have social anxiety you are likely to:

☐ Assume others know the right way to do things
☐ Assume you are the only one who doesn't know the right answers or who has ever made a mistake learning something new
☐ Believe that you will be rejected in new situations
☐ Assume that other people are watching you when you are in public
☐ Believe that feeling humiliated is inevitable and you won't be able to get over it

Of the 15 items above, how many did you check? If you checked:

2 or fewer = You do not have social anxiety disorder. Everyone feels these things from time to time.
3 = You are probably holding back from situations.
4 or more = You are too worried about your social acceptability and may be suffering social anxiety. The techniques in this book will help you desensitize yourself and unlearn fear.

Performance anxiety is a form of social anxiety. It is when you have one specific social situation that gives you anxiety—such as singing in public, giving a speech, auditioning, or standing up in a classroom. Your anxiety may be intense enough to make you avoid that situation at all costs, but it is restricted to that one kind of situation. There are many treatments—such as energy therapies and EMDR—that can help you overcome performance anxiety. See the Recommended Reading & Resources section at the end of the book.

SPECIFIC PHOBIA

A phobia is a fear of a specific thing, like snakes, spiders, or insects. Many people suffer phobias, which usually cause only minor interference with life. However, some specific phobias—like fear of the dark, driving over a bridge, or claustrophobia—can be debilitating because they interfere with many life situations.

Some phobias do not seem related to any specific event that started the fear. These can usually be treated fairly easily with any of several desensitization methods. When the phobia is the outcome of a traumatic experience, the right treatment depends on the type of event and the kinds of repercussions still present in your life.

POST-TRAUMATIC STRESS DISORDER

Over the past decade, as combat veterans have struggled to reintegrate into civilian life, post-traumatic stress disorder (PTSD) has received a lot of well-deserved attention in the press. PTSD is a serious condition, the result of an experience:

- That threatened your life or the life of someone else in your presence
- That created a sense of terror
- In which you were not in control, such as a natural disaster, war, or crime

Not everyone gets PTSD as a result of such experiences, but when people of any age have had such an experience, they may begin to experience serious symptoms that disrupt their lives and wellbeing. They may have nightmares or flashbacks in which they reexperience all or part of the trauma. They may become depressed or anxious, have trouble concentrating or sleeping, and become easily agitated or even angry and rageful. These symptoms usually appear about a month after the event, but sometimes they don't occur for many months or even years. Although all of the techniques discussed in this book will help manage symptoms of the anxiety accompanying PTSD, they won't resolve the traumatic experience. If you suffer PTSD or suspect that you do, consult a therapist. Help is available!

OBSESSIVE-COMPULSIVE DISORDER

Unlike the other anxiety disorders, obsessive-compulsive disorder (OCD) is not caused by life events. You can teach people to worry too much or be too cautious, but you cannot teach them to be compulsive hand-washers, checkers, or hoarders. OCD is a neurobiological problem that people are born with, though it may not emerge until adolescence or adulthood. Why it emerges at a certain age is not well understood, but some OCD may be triggered by strep infections that are not sufficiently treated.

The signs of OCD include unreasonable worries and fears that are obsessive. These obsessive thoughts may cause a person to develop ritualistic behaviors ("compulsions") to try to relieve the anxiety caused by the obsessive thought.

Some compulsions, like repeated hand-washing, are obvious, but others are much more subtle, such as touching a talisman or leaving the house on the same foot every time you walk out.

People with OCD are stricken with uncertainty that they have completed the task, and this sense of incompleteness leads them to do the behavior over and over. Some obsessions do not include rituals, but involve counting, organizing in the mind, or scrupulously reciting prayers. Adults may not be able to control their behavior but know their obsessions and compulsions are unrealistic. Children are often unaware that their ideas are unrealistic and may not voluntarily bring them to your attention.

The techniques in this book that involve calming down physiology will help people with OCD, but the cognitive techniques are not well suited to treatment of the disorder. Go to the Obsessive-Compulsive Foundation website (see the Recommended Reading and Resources section) for signs, symptoms, and ideas for treatment.

COEXISTING CONDITIONS

Some common mental-health conditions can cause anxiety or intensify anxiety, and they confuse the picture as to whether a discrete anxiety disorder exists. There are three in particular that should be mentioned: attention-deficit disorder, with or without hyperactivity (ADD, ADHD); Asperger's disorder; and addiction, especially alcoholism.

Attention-Deficit Disorder

People who have ADD often feel anxious about the way their problems with attention interfere with remembering, following through, or completing work assignments or schoolwork. Children who have academic difficulties are screened for ADD and other learning disabilities (LD), but not all people with ADD do poorly academically and, thus, do not come to the attention of the school for LD screening. Their ADD may go unrecognized for a long time. People with ADD may suffer considerable, legitimate worry about whether they have taken care of necessary tasks or noticed everything they should notice. Because they often have trouble organizing, finding workable methods to help track responsibilities is a challenge. They are prone to time-gobbling accidents of spilling, breaking, or losing things. Fearing they have made mistakes is not unreasonable, but the worry can grow to uncontrollable proportions. The best remedy for anxiety about the real problems created by ADD is actively treating the disorder with strategies and medication when appropriate.

Do You Need an ADD/ADHD Evaluation?

Even if you were not diagnosed with ADD in childhood, it may be a good idea to be screened if you begin to suffer anxiety and have some of the indicators in the following lists (the first is for adolescents; the second is for adults). In people who have done well academically, the appearance of anxiety at times of life transitions warrants careful attention.

Do You Have ADD?

Are you an adolescent who has done well in school (at least until now) and are currently:

☐ Applying for college and feeling overwhelmed by the choices of where to go

☐ Applying for college but avoiding the confusing demands of the applications (essays, collecting documents and recommendations, submitting resumes, or answering questions)

☐ Taking AP classes and feeling overwhelmed by the assignments or expectations (you may be feeling test anxiety for the first time)

☐ Doing a new responsibility—such as editing the yearbook, participating in student council, being a team captain or an officer in a school organization—and feeling panicked about the duties

☐ Recently doing part-time work in addition to school and feeling overwhelmed by keeping the schedule straight and getting all your work done

Adolescents who checked any of the above questions should get an ADD screening.

In their online newsletter, *Harvard Health Publications* stated: "The profile of an adult with ADHD can vary from that of a child. Most experts agree that pure hyperactive behavior usually diminishes with maturity. Adults usually have problems with time management, self-control, planning for the future, and being able to persist toward goals" (2004; see www.health.harvard.edu/press_releases/adult_adhd_treatment).

Do You Have ADD?

Are you an adult who has become exceedingly anxious (panicky, worried, or both) and has also:

- ☐ Historically been disorganized at work and relied on colleagues or assistants to get the organization done
- ☐ Failed to complete tasks, regardless of whether you enjoy the work
- ☐ Been hyperfocused on certain things, like video games, that stimulate you
- ☐ Avoided jobs that require you to complete paperwork or organize environments
- ☐ Avoided reading, especially texts and manuals, and preferred to learn new information by doing the task
- ☐ Done very well in your work until you got promoted and now feel incompetent or worried about losing your job
- ☐ Recently become a parent and begun to feel as if everything is overwhelming and too much to keep track of, despite your having done very well in your job and managed home life until now
- ☐ Found yourself, after a change in work or home duties, being suddenly forgetful and missing appointments, deadlines, or phone calls that you previously might have managed
- ☐ Saying way too much and then wishing you had more restraint

If you checked any two of the criteria above, you should take a screening test for ADD and seek ADD treatment in addition to anxiety management.

In my clinical experience, when people with ADD are intelligent and do well academically, they do not come to the attention of the school as having learning problems. But they may suffer intense anxiety about making mistakes, which they legitimately make but cannot figure out how to avoid. They may not cross this threshold until the responsibility they take on exceeds whatever strategies they developed to manage the ADD without realizing they were managing it. Then they worry about their competency or ability to succeed. If you are not achieving what you know you are capable of, feeling anxiety about competency even though you are stably employed, or having difficulty keeping your home organized despite making an effort, you might want to consider whether ADD may be playing a role in this.

Parents of adolescents assume the teen's anxiety is related to separation from home to attend college or to taking classes that are too difficult, and they want the adolescent to have anxiety/stress management and homework strategies. In these cases anxiety management requires managing ADD and then learning to calm the physiology and manage worry.

If you think you may have ADD, see www.add.org for a host of reliable resources for screening and treatment. Also check out the Harvard Medical School screening tool for adult attention-deficit disorder.

Asperger's Disorder

Estimates of children with symptoms on the autism-disorder spectrum range from 1 in 110 to 1 in 150 children in the United States. Asperger's disorder, which affects the development of language and social skills, is on the autism spectrum, though it is much milder in its impairments. In high-functioning individuals, Asperger's symptoms can be mistaken for social anxiety. Those symptoms may include:

- Sensitivity to environmental stimulation
- Social awkwardness and lack of responsiveness to emotional signals from others
- Body language or vocalization that is "off"—not exactly matching the words or social circumstance
- Indirect or very brief eye contact
- Intense, narrow interests
- Physical clumsiness
- Behavior seen by peers as "odd"

The key to differentiating Asperger's disorder from social anxiety lies in examining the individual's interest in and ability to relate to others. Socially anxious children and young adults may be very interested in friendships and able to interact but uncertain or embarrassed about their lack of social experience or shyness. Although they prefer one-on-one interactions or small groups, they can learn to participate with groups in activities they enjoy, such as sports. They clearly understand social signals though they may be overreactive to negative signals. The child with Asperger's, on the other hand, may want to interact with others but have trouble reading social signals correctly. These children need specific instruction about how to recognize social signals and how to show socially appropriate responses.

A major challenge for people with Asperger's is their difficulty with changing: changing the topic of discussion, changing the activity, changing their location, or changing any routine. For them, safety is in knowing what to expect and how to react, so in new situations they may feel intense anxiety and thus make efforts to avoid new and unfamiliar circumstances. People with social anxiety may also avoid what is new or unfamiliar but for a different reason: They do not want to be observed making mistakes or looking embarrassed, which could result in being rejected by others. They would be happy to learn new things if they were not being observed while doing so. And whereas people with Asperger's have difficulty identifying what others think, feel, or are interested in, socially anxious people are overly tuned in to others, overestimating the degree of disapproval they might experience.

Because Asperger's makes forming successful connections with others difficult, young people with the disorder may develop anxiety or depression. However, interventions to help children develop communication and social skills are effective at improving a child's ability to thrive, and the earlier those interventions can be started, the more effective they are at improving development in those areas.

It is suggested by the American Academy of Pediatrics (www.aap.org) that all children get screened for the autism spectrum at 18 months of age. A new study by Drs. Chris Johnson and Scott Myers has produced a screening questionnaire for pediatricians that is simple and reliable.

Addiction

Many people with anxiety turn to alcohol to calm themselves, which can lead to alcohol abuse or addiction, because habitual use can become a problem for some. Another issue is how to recognize and treat anxiety disorder if you are an alcoholic in recovery. Anxiety can lead to relapsing if you are not managing your anxiety symptoms.

If you are in recovery from alcohol addiction, managing your anxiety may require more than your addiction-treatment program or 12-step self-help program (both of which I believe in!) can provide. Do not regard it as a treatment failure if you need more strategies than addiction recovery to deal with anxiety. Your anxiety may have predated the addiction, even if you didn't recognize it. But once anxiety is present, it needs to be managed!

The issue of addiction is too big to address here except in the broadest strokes. Here are some bullet points:

- Stimulant abuse can trigger anxiety that persists into recovery.
- You may develop addiction if you use marijuana, alcohol, food, or the Internet to handle anxiety or social fears.
- Alcohol causes a rebound to more intense anxiety. If you slip in recovery, the subsequent anxiety may be due to more than just your worries about the relapse.
- Addiction may both calm anxiety and *cause* it, as financial, interpersonal, health, and legal issues surrounding addiction begin to mount.

If you are in recovery, do not underestimate the power of anxiety to interfere with your progress. Seek help to manage anxiety rather than risk relapse. For those of you with anxiety who are abusing substances or behaviors, anxiety treatment may be the start of recovery.

RESOURCES

The Recommended Reading and Resources section at the end of this book lists many websites and books that can provide more information on anxiety and related problems. If you have questions about your symptoms and wonder whether you might have anxiety, there are several excellent self-tests on the website of the Anxiety Disorder Association of America (www.adaa.org). You should be aware that many web resources offer free self-tests, but most also want to sell you a program for self-help. A good evaluation by a skilled professional should be the next step after self-testing on the Internet.

Anxiety disorders can be treated by a wide range of mental-health professionals, most typically psychologists, clinical social workers, and counselors.

Although all psychiatrists and most primary-care physicians will prescribe medication for anxiety, they do not usually offer the therapy to teach you techniques that control anxious symptoms. That's where therapists come in.

Choosing a Therapist

If you seek help from a therapist, which is often a good idea, it's best to find someone who is oriented to helping you diminish symptoms of anxiety as well as work through underlying psychological issues. Finding the right therapist is not always easy, as many competent therapists with good credentials do not always practice the pragmatic style of thought and behavior management that works best with anxiety symptoms. Ask your doctor for a referral or look on the Anxiety Disorder Association of America website (www.adaa.org) for a list of therapists in your area who belong to the association. Therapists who specialize in trauma treatment are also likely to have experience treating anxiety. Eye movement desensitization and reprocessing (EMDR) is a form of therapy that uses a technique called "dual attention stimulus" (such as alternate hand-tapping) to help resolve symptoms resulting from disturbing, unresolved life experiences. Visit the EMDR International Association website (www.emdria.org) for a list of therapists who are trained in that method in your area.

When you find a therapist in your area, ask to speak to that person before you schedule an appointment. Do not hesitate to ask questions about the therapist's training, style of working, and relevant details about the therapy sessions (times, cost, etc.) These questions don't require long answers or explanations, and a therapist who treats anxiety well will be able to respond quickly to them.

Questions to Ask

Following are some questions and guidelines to use when seeking a therapist to treat your anxiety.

- What training and experience do you have in treating anxiety?
  You might also ask some of these questions:
  - What is your therapy approach to anxiety? (Ask about your type of anxiety.)

- What kinds of cognitive techniques do you use?
- Do you give "homework" assignments?
- What methods might you recommend for panic attacks?

• What do you believe about the need to get rid of underlying causes of anxiety in order to get rid of symptoms? You should get an answer that suggests:
  - Symptom management may be possible without long-term work, *and*
  - If anxiety is caused by unresolved issues (such as a previous trauma), it will come back unless the person deals with those issues.

• How frequently will you expect to see me, and how long does one session last?

• Do you include family members in treatment?
  - If seeking help for a child, parents must be included.
  - It is a good idea for a spouse or partner to hear about the biological nature of anxiety and to learn from the therapist how to respond to the complaints of anxiety that come up at home.

• What is your fee schedule?
  - Ask for details about insurance coverage, sliding fees, and so on.
  - Ask about community resources for special financial circumstances.

Remember, if a therapist is skilled in treating anxiety, his or her answers to these questions should be clear and direct. Any therapist who is vague or reluctant to answer your questions may not have the skills you need to improve your anxiety rapidly.

TREATMENT OPTIONS

There are three prongs involved in anxiety treatment: techniques that focus on the body, techniques that focus on the mind (cognition), and techniques that focus on behavior. Some types of techniques are better than others for certain kinds of anxiety—for example, those that focus on the body are best for panic disorder—but generally speaking, a combination of all three types is most effective.

The following treatment options are the most commonly used for anxiety.

Relaxation Techniques

Relaxation techniques, such as diaphragmatic breathing and progressive muscle relaxation, help individuals to diminish physical symptoms of anxiety, and you can learn and practice these techniques on your own. Relaxation and other techniques that target physical symptoms are described in Chapters 3–6 of this book and provided on the CD.

Cognitive-Behavioral Therapy

Cognitive-behavioral therapy (CBT) identifies anxious patterns of both thought and behavior that keep unwanted symptoms in place. Using CBT methods, which are learned in therapy sessions, people can begin to cope with anxiety-producing situations and control thoughts and behaviors that keep anxiety in place or harm them socially and emotionally. Individuals are at all times involved in planning and practicing techniques for their recovery.

Chapters 7–9 of this book offer techniques that focus on the mind, and Chapters 10–12 include techniques that target behavior. You can learn and use these techniques on your own, but they may be more effective if you also seek the help of a therapist trained in CBT.

Medication

Medication is often used in conjunction with psychotherapy. It is often not necessary but may be very helpful. The typical medication choices include the selective serotonin reuptake inhibitors (SSRIs, which are often confusingly called "antidepressants") and limited use of benzodiazepines for anxiety reduction.

A FINAL WORD

Anxiety disorders are treatable. Treatment varies with the type of anxiety and whether a person experiences more than one kind of anxiety. Improvement in physical symptoms, such as panic, may occur fairly quickly (perhaps within a few months), whereas diminishing persistent worry may take longer. Treatment is always geared to individual situations: what type of anxiety you have, how long the condition has lasted, what kinds of life situations affect you, and so on. No single plan works for everyone.

The goal of this workbook is to help all anxiety sufferers, regardless of whether you are also getting help from a professional. If you have success using the techniques presented here without the help of a professional guide, good for you! But if you still find yourself struggling even after trying the techniques, do not give up. It is likely that all you need is the guidance of a psychotherapist to make these 10 best-ever anxiety management techniques work for you.

TWO

Assess Your Stress: Understanding How Your Stress Level Affects Anxiety

Many people talk about being "stressed out" and "feeling stressed." Most of us know what the general expression implies. However, stress is a physical and emotional state that has diverse symptoms, and it can create big problems if you do not recognize and respond to it well. It can create or magnify anxiety and deplete your resources to deal with it.

Before we look at stress specifically, you should have a bit of knowledge about brain science. You don't need to know brain science to be able to effectively use the techniques in this book, but understanding it at least a little helps. The following section covers the basics; for a more in-depth discussion of brain science, see my books *The 10 Best-Ever Anxiety Managements Techniques* and *The Anxious Brain*.

BRAIN BASICS

All of our emotional reactions are experienced physically and mentally. Your brain sets those reactions in motion when you experience stimulation from the world around you, from inside of yourself, or when your thoughts prompt emotion. Although all the parts of your brain should work smoothly in concert with each other, certain parts of the brain have specific functions. Deep in the center of the brain you have a system for instant recognition of signals from the world around you. It is called the limbic system. It immediately notes the importance and quality of those signals without putting any words to the situation. A smile or a frown, a siren or a chime—any kind of signal comes with an emotional tone. You will immediately have a physical change, faster than you can think, based on how this system assesses the signal.

Another part of your brain—the one you consciously think with—is slower to respond (although it still responds pretty darned fast!) and what you think about the signal is colored by the way your body is responding. In this front and center part of the brain, you gather the information together, think things over, and make decisions about whether the emotional response makes sense or should be changed somehow. An example of this might be the process of getting mad but cooling off when you realize the other person did not mean to insult you, or feeling nervous about meeting someone new but then thinking the person is really quite friendly and consequently feeling less nervous.

All of those processes are conducted by electrical signals and chemical messengers (neurotransmitters) that carry specific kinds of messages depending on where in the brain they are active. Medications affect the chemical messages, but the good news—and the reason the techniques in this workbook will work—is that we can deliberately change the message by using the "thinking" part of our brain. Ultimately that will change the ways the messengers work, promoting better functioning of your brain.

Now let's look at how stress affects the brain and body.

WHAT IS HAPPENING WHEN YOU ARE STRESSED?

Your body reacts to challenges via two physiological systems: the "fight or flight" response and the "stress response." Both responses are active when you experience a stressful event. You've probably already heard of the "fight or flight" response. This is the automatic physical response that occurs when you get worked up emotionally, mentally, or physically. If you have to run to catch a bus, you don't *decide* to have increased respiration or heart rate. This automatic function works without conscious thought. Your nervous system increases your heart rate, blood pressure, and respiration, changes blood flow, and generally makes sure you are ready to move physically. Whether you are climbing stairs (you need more energy *now*) or listening to a parent yelling (a possible threat indicating that you just *might* need to move fast), this system goes to work. It is called the "fight or flight" response because it prepares you to do just that—run away from danger

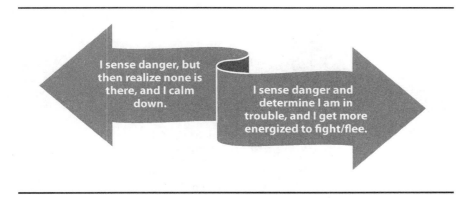

Figure 2.1 Thinking Controls Automatic Fight or Flight

I sense danger, but then realize none is there, and I calm down.

I sense danger and determine I am in trouble, and I get more energized to fight/flee.

or protect yourself from it. If you need to make a *big* response to a challenge, your body has to be ready.

How does this automatic system get turned on? It's triggered by the fast-acting amygdala in the limbic system of your brain, which is always alert and scanning for danger. If it notices anything in the world around you that is a potential risk to your safety, your body responds immediately so you are ready to act, even before you have time to think. For example, if a siren goes off, you immediately have a burst of "fight or flight" in case you have to get out of there. Once you have time to think and your thinking prefrontal cortex decides there is no need to worry or act, this arousal settles back down. If your thinking brain says there is danger, however, the arousal remains or intensifies. Figure 2.1 illustrates this.

Fight or Flight and Anxiety

If you have panic or anxiety, it may start with a physical feeling—even though no real danger exists. Your brain does not like it when you have a physical sensation without an observable reason, so it decides, "If I feel this bad, there must be something wrong!" Your helpful brain starts to look around for a reason you're having a racing heart or shallow breathing, and it's usually good at tricking itself into thinking it's found one. For example, if you have that kind of sensation while entering your first big lecture class in college, or driving on the highway in heavy traffic, or meeting new colleagues for the first time, your brain might

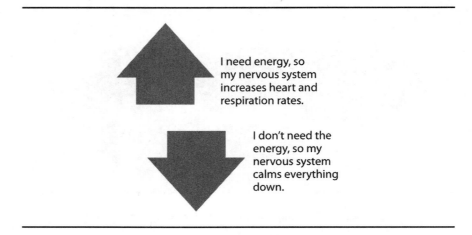

Figure 2.2 Your Body Is Either Getting Aroused or Calming Down

decide that the activity *caused* the burst of fight or flight energy. And once it decides that, you might be inclined to avoid that situation in the future in an attempt to avoid feeling bad.

The good news about the arousal response is that you cannot become aroused and calm down at the same time: You are either working up to "fight or flight" or calming it down, as depicted in Figure 2.2. This is the physical reality that underlies control of panic. You can use the calming system to decrease all the negative symptoms of a panic attack.

If you feel physical energy but you interpret it as a good thing, such as anticipation of fun, sexual excitement, or the outcome of physical exercise, you won't be disturbed. Your brain knows something good is the cause. But when that non-thinking alarm goes off—saying "look out!"—you will go on the alert, and your heart rate will increase. If it is mild, you might be able to ignore it, but if you are in danger and you know you are, you will have a sudden, intense arousal of the "fight or flight" system. That is appropriate to help you respond to the danger and get to safety. The outcome is depicted in Figure 2.3.

When this sudden acceleration happens *in the absence of* real danger, it's called a panic attack. Your heart can go up to 200 beats a minute and your breath can get short and shallow, even panting. Your nervous system gives you a jolt of adrenalin, so that you will have the readiness to fight hard or run fast. It is men-

The 10 Best-Ever Anxiety Management Techniques Workbook

Figure 2.3 Fight or Flight Arousal Prepares You for Action

tally disconcerting to be that aroused without knowing the reason, and you may fear that you are dying, going crazy, or losing control when you have a panic attack. The feeling of dying is so real that many people rush to the hospital, sure they are having a heart attack.

When a panic attack is over a person can be left feeling jangled and exhausted. Even though the average panic attack peaks after only 11 to 13 minutes, the aftermath can last for hours. One particularly disturbing outcome of a panic attack is that you may have a persistent sensation that something bad is happening or will happen. This feeling may last for hours and can be hard to shake off. One of my clients, Glenda, gave an excellent example of this. She was driving on a snowy day when her car was hit by another car skidding on the slippery road. She felt a jolt of shock and panicked for a few minutes, until she realized there was no injury and her car was drivable, despite noticeable rear-end damage. Later that evening, though, she began to feel sick. Her heart rate was only slightly elevated and her breathing was normal, but she couldn't shake the feeling that something was wrong. So she began to think that she was having the feeling because she had neglected to make a police report and only took insurance information. Then she spent the night trying to figure out what would happen: She imagined that failure to call the police would result in an insurance denial of the claim, and her husband would be furious, and it would cost more money than she could afford, and so on and so on until she was emotionally tied in knots. Her imagined fears explained her gut feeling but they did not help get rid of it—in fact, they made it worse. All because her stomach told her something was wrong. The feeling in her gut was just the aftermath of the panic. Glenda needed to instead tell herself that nothing was wrong and work on distraction and calming rather than explaining.

The Stress Response

Panic may drive people to the hospital thinking they are about to die, but it is being under stress that is the real killer. Yet few people rush to the hospital when they feel stress. The stress response is an endocrinological response that gives your brain and body the energy it needs to run or fight. When that alarm goes off, your pituitary gland sends a signal through your bloodstream to your adrenal glands to release adrenalin and cortisol for mobilizing energy. This is a bit slower than the initial electric jolt of "fight or flight" that calls for a burst of adrenalin for immediate energy, and it can go on for quite some time. The adrenalin increases the intensity of heartbeat and respiration. The cortisol tells your body to release fat and glucose for burning up if you are fighting or running. Cortisol is also the brake. When your brain receives cortisol in the bloodstream, it knows the "STRESS!" message has been received and stops requesting stress response. You can see this feedback loop in Figure 2.4.

Under stress your brain reacts, too, releasing supplies of neurotransmitters that help you respond. The neurotransmitters that regulate mood and cognition are especially affected. The stress response is dose-specific. If you have a small

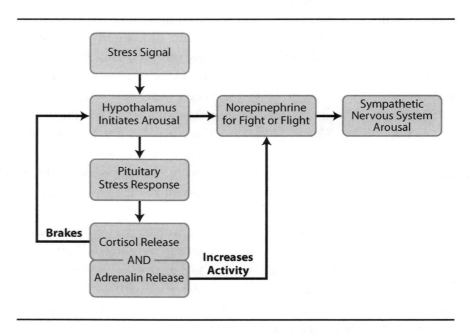

Figure 2.4 The Endocrinological Stress Response

The 10 Best-Ever Anxiety Management Techniques Workbook

stress and only need a little energy, you will get a small stress response. If the stress goes on for a long time, you will get stress response until you do not need it anymore. In other words, the duration and intensity of the stress response are determined by what kind of stress you are experiencing. And therein lies the problem. Stress response over a period of a few minutes, like during panic, is not all that troubling physically. But stress response of any intensity over a period of time becomes a physical and emotional challenge.

There are several things that happen to your detriment when stress is on-going:

- If your energy supply is not burned off through physical exertion, such as when sitting in front of a computer 12 hours a day working to keep your business from going under, you have a release of energy that never gets used. This is a major reason people put fat on in their middles when under stress.
- Ongoing release of adrenalin can result in adrenal fatigue, causing problems with immune functions.
- Immune activity is suppressed when you are stressed for a long period, so you may end up getting sick.
- Worse, intense and ongoing stress can lead to diseases and conditions that you are genetically susceptible to, such as diabetes type II, heart disease, or autoimmune disorders.
- If stress is severe and ongoing, the impact of all that cortisol hitting your brain can affect your ability to remember things.
- You may end up so depleted of neurotransmitters that you become depressed or anxious.

Being "stressed out" is not just a momentary unpleasantness—it is a serious health risk. And the impact on anxiety is direct. Not only do the specific conditions creating stress affect you, but the change in your health and mental functioning due to the imbalance of neurotransmitters and the other physical changes may create sensations of anxiety. Feeling anxious, you may then start to worry—a natural response to feelings of anxiety. Once your sensation of anxiety triggers worrying, you then have a feedback loop in which the anxiety and worry make each other worse, creating even more stress! (See Chapters 7–9 for techniques to control worry.)

QUANTITY AND QUALITY OF STRESS

Hint: Stress is subjective. If you feel it, you should deal with it. Change the situation or change your self-care!

There are two types of ongoing stress. One is related to *quantity* of stress—when we have more to do than we can actually accomplish in the time we have available. For example, perhaps you have been given extra responsibilities at work, or feel pressured to take on extra responsibilities that you cannot reasonably handle. Or perhaps you are a parent who works outside of the home and must care for children when you get home after work. Single mothers are particularly vulnerable to this stress. When living with quantity stress, people tend to stop exercising, sleep too little, and stop cooking at home because the time demands seem too intense to maintain that level of self-care.

The other kind of stress has to do with its *quality*. There are times when we are under stress that is emotionally charged, such as when:

- We are caring for a loved one who is chronically or terminally ill
- Someone we love has died, and for months or longer we not only grieve but also have to handle legal matters or medical bills that keep resurrecting the trauma of losing that person
- We have no control or ability to protect a loved one who is in trouble or in danger, such as soldiers at war or people on trial or in jail
- We are struggling to make ends meet financially and worried about how it will work out
- We suffer from oppression and poverty (people with few resources, like those who are still trying to rebuild after natural disasters, suffer from this heartrending and inescapable kind of stress)

People with quality stress typically feel too emotionally drained to take care of themselves well.

Whether it is quality stress or quantity stress, the lack of control you feel makes the situation feel stressful. This feeling of lack of control may stem from a very real lack of resources to correct problems, but it also can result from misperceptions. For example, you may not like your job and feel that you *must* stay at that job because if you don't, you won't have an income. You feel like you don't have a choice about it, but in truth you do—you are *choosing* the income. Seeing that you have a choice makes a big difference.

ADOLESCENTS AND STRESS

I am completely appalled at the schedules kept by many children and adolescents and equally shocked by how many parents refuse to give their children free or unscheduled time. Both teens and parents seem to believe that if they don't do every activity possible, they might miss the one and only opportunity to discover a talent or get a scholarship or entry into a good school. When I see adolescents with anxiety, I find it helpful to assess how much they are doing that they genuinely want to do versus how much they are doing because they are complying with external pressure. The following chart may help adolescents or college students see whether they have choice. Recognizing that they personally have good reasons for doing something, even if an authority also wants them to do it, can reduce the pressure. And if they are only doing it to please another person, it might be time to make a change.

Do I Have a Choice?		
What Do I Do? (list all activities)	My Reasons for Doing These Activities	My Parents', Coach's, or Teachers' Reasons

HOW STRESSFUL IS YOUR LIFE?

Panic is not good for your body or your mental state, but it is not nearly as damaging as ongoing stress. So evaluate your stress here and then pay careful attention to the lifestyle changes discussed in Chapters 3–6.

How Stressful Is Your Life?

Give yourself the number of points indicated for items that apply to you.

Changes at work:

____ Change in type of work or major change in job expectations (1)

____ Change in coworkers (2)

____ Change in boss or supervisor (3)

____ Change in career (4)

Score _____

Changes in living:

____ Moved to a new home within same city (1)

____ Moved to a different city within same country (2)

____ Moved to another country (3)

Score _____

Changes in finances:

____ Took a cut in pay (1)

____ Living in a more expensive area (2)

____ Sending children to a more expensive school (3)

____ Have incurred credit-card debt that cannot be quickly paid off (4)

____ Took a new mortgage (5)

Score ____

Changes in personal life:

____ Began a new important relationship (1)

____ Believe your personal life must be kept private for your wellbeing at work (2)

____ Got married (3)

____ Had a child (4)

____ Living separately from your spouse who is in another location (5)

____ Living with a person who creates serious problems for your wellbeing (e.g., is persistently verbally berating, is often emotionally distraught and shows it in tearful, angry, or frightening outbursts, or is addicted to substances and you must interact with that person while he or she is under the influence and put up with the person's stealing, accidents, or physical consequences of the addiction) (6)

Score _____

Changes in health:
_____ Had a short-term illness that caused you to miss a few days of work (2)
_____ Are undergoing tests to determine cause of symptoms, without positive tests (4)
_____ Had a serious illness that caused you to miss many days of work (6)
_____ Have a chronic illness that affects your energy and overall feeling of wellness (8)
_____ Have a newly diagnosed, serious chronic illness that is not terminal (10)
Score _____

Losses:
(*Note: It is difficult to numerically rate the emotional upset caused by losses. For example, a person who has relied on a service dog may grieve the loss of that animal as a beloved family member, whereas someone without a strong feeling toward a family pet may bounce back quickly. Likewise, the loss of an extended family member could be experienced as grievous or only mild. Furthermore, emotional and financial support resources—or lack thereof—may have an effect. If you have experienced any of the following losses, rate it on a scale of 1 to 13, with 1 being very mild loss and 13 being grievous loss.*)
_____ Loss of a beloved pet
_____ Diminishing health of a parent for whom you provide some care
_____ Living with a parent or child with serious, chronic health problems
_____ Death of a mother, father, or sibling
_____ Death of a child
_____ Death of an extended family member
_____ Death of a friend or coworker
_____ Death of a spouse
_____ Divorce
_____ Loss of home due to foreclosure
_____ Loss of job
Score _____

Total of all Scores _____

1–9 points = Stress in your life is happening. Maintain good self-care, as always.
10–12 points = Yellow caution zone. Stress is taking a toll and you need to pay special attention to replenishing your energy so you do not become exhausted.
13 points or more = Red zone. Reach out for help and support. This is when people tend to get sick or have accidents. Be especially careful about sleep and nutrition, take your vitamins, and seek and accept help of all types wherever it is available.

Every stressful period can result in growth or loss, depending on how you care for yourself during this time. But if too many stresses pile up and you do not get assistance or take care of yourself, you may suffer losses in relationships and in physical and mental wellbeing. If you are the type of person who tends to take on way too much responsibility and downplays the effect stress is having in your life, pay particular attention to the techniques in Chapter 11.

Has It Already Gone on Too Long?

Are you showing signs of destructive stress? Take this test to see if you have indications that stress is negatively affecting you.

Is Stress Negatively Affecting You?

Check off the physical signs of stress that you are experiencing regularly:

- ☐ Headaches
- ☐ Muscle pain, especially back pain
- ☐ Indigestion
- ☐ Diarrhea
- ☐ Appetite changes
- ☐ Jaw tightening, tooth grinding, TMJ
- ☐ Weakness and fatigue
- ☐ Insomnia

Check off the emotional signs of stress that are you experiencing regularly:

- ☐ Become irritable or grouchy over little things
- ☐ Are easily angered
- ☐ Feel anxiety that you cannot resolve
- ☐ Feel as if everything that might have been fun is now a burden to do
- ☐ Frequent loss of concentration
- ☐ Making more mistakes in work than usual
- ☐ Becoming accident prone
- ☐ Feeling frozen about where to start each day or each activity

Check off the signs of poor self-care that are you experiencing regularly:

- ☐ Stopped exercise regimens
- ☐ Eating more food or more junk food
- ☐ Experiencing weight gain, especially around your middle
- ☐ Drinking more alcohol to relax
- ☐ Drinking more caffeine for energy to get going in the morning
- ☐ Not dressing with as much care
- ☐ Paying less attention to personal appearance, like tidy clothing or makeup
- ☐ Decrease in leisure time and pleasant contact with friends or family

Total Items Checked: _____

0–3 = You are sailing along without serious effects of stress and should teach others how you do it!

4–5 = Stress is starting to interfere with health or wellbeing. Take some self-care steps.

6–8 = Reevaluate now! Stress is affecting your wellbeing.

8 or more = Talk to someone immediately about how to diminish stress today.

A FINAL WORD

Once you have a sense of the stress you are experiencing, you may find that you are stymied in changing the level of stress. I have found that when people have serious life stress, they lose perspective and may need an outside person to help them see ways to decrease their level of stress or get some help. The good news is that proper self-care will help alleviate the negative impact of stress.

Pay careful attention to your nutrition, exercise, and sleep. See my book *The 10 Best-Ever Anxiety Management Techniques* for a longer discussion of those needs, and check out the Recommended Reading and Resources section of this book.

PART II

Managing the Anxious Body

THREE

Technique #1: Change Your Intake

Changing intake—from the kinds of food you eat to how often you check email—is a key feature in managing the physiology of anxiety. Whether you have panic attacks, acute anxiety, or that sick feeling of having made a social gaffe, you feel anxiety in your body. These physical feelings can be triggered by something as simple as drinking a cup of coffee—but your brain doesn't always recognize this. It may instead jump to the conclusion that you are having these physical sensations because there is something very real that you need to be worried about, and it will begin making up reasons to explain why you feel so physically anxious. This chapter will help your brain notice the connection between intake and feelings of anxiety or panic.

ASSESS YOUR INTAKE OF C.A.T.S.

C.A.T.S. stands for caffeine, alcohol, tobacco, and sugar and sweeteners. If you have the physical sensations of anxiety, the first step of assessment (after you consult a physician) is to assess your level of C.A.T.S. intake.

Track Anxiety Related to Caffeine and Sugar/Sweeteners

The first appraisal is easy: Write down what you eat and drink, and then set a timer for 45 minutes and check how you feel. Are caffeine, sugar, or other specific foods triggering anxiety sensations? One of my clients, Eleanor, was surprised to find that her anxiety was very predictable: If she ate sugar, like candy or any type of dessert, without also having other food, a sensation of intense dread would follow within an hour.

Because sensitivity varies greatly from person to person, only you can tell whether certain foods and drinks are causing your anxiety symptoms. The best way to do this is by tracking how you feel after eating or drinking. You may also note that some foods produce feelings other than anxiety: You may feel sleepy, jittery, energized, mellow, alert, and so on. That might help you assess the impact of your food intake in general.

Use the following chart to track the foods and drinks you consume, and then rate your anxiety (or panic) levels on a scale of 1 to 10, with 1 being low and 10 intense. A sample chart is provided first (Figure 3.1), with a blank one for you to fill out after that (you can also use an index card or your smartphone to keep track). Make sure you track your intake over several days so you can identify any consistent effects on your anxiety or panic.

> Hint: If you want reasonable nutritional guidelines, check out the website www.health.gov/dietaryguidelines/dga2005/toolkit

Anxiety/Panic Before and After Food and Drink Consumption

Rate your anxiety/panic from 1 to 10, with 1 being low and 10 intense.

Level of Anxiety/Panic Before I Eat	What I Ate/Drank	Level of Anxiety/Panic 45 Minutes After I Eat
3 – a little worried feeling	large coffee with cream	7 – feeling like something's wrong
4 – not back to morning level	hot dog and fries	3 – busy at work so am distracted from worry
3 – still distracted from thoughts	large cola	8 – feels like dread now, but the boss asked me to stay late
5 – but I worked late and rushed home	fish filet, green beans, and brown rice; water/decaf tea	3 – feel calmer but still worried about how much work I have

Figure 3.1 Anxiety/Panic Before and After Food and Drink Consumption

Anxiety/Panic Before and After Food and Drink Consumption

Rate your anxiety/panic from 1 to 10, with 1 being low and 10 intense.

Level of Anxiety/Panic Before I Eat	What I Ate/Drank	Level of Anxiety/Panic 45 Minutes After I Eat

Notes: _____

_____

_____

_____

Track Anxiety Related to Alcohol

Many people use alcohol to calm down, and that may work. But alcohol can cause problems with anxiety, panic, and restless sleep. Even a relatively small amount of alcohol may disrupt your sleep pattern, and this lack of sleep can contribute to anxiety. Drinking to the point of drunkenness, as many young adults do, can lead to problems not only with anxiety but also with alcohol dependence.

Is alcohol contributing to your panic or anxiety? Keep a "Day After" Diary to find out. Every time you consume alcohol, note how much you are drinking and the time of day. In the morning, rate your quality of sleep on a scale from 1 (excellent) to 10 (poor). At the

Hint: If you are worried about your alcohol consumption (which could make you anxious!) then go online and take a free test to evaluate your use. Try the Michigan Alcohol Screening Test (MAST) or the CAGE Questionnaire, both of which are free, or go to the website for Alcoholics Anonymous.

end of the day, rate the intensity of anxiety (or occurrence of panic attacks) you experienced throughout the day, again using a scale of 1 (low intensity) to 10 (high intensity). Do this for several occasions of using alcohol to see if there is consistent pattern. Then decide if you want to stop using alcohol in that way.

Alcohol Intake "Day After" Diary

In the left-hand column, note the number of drinks you had and the time of day you consumed them. In the middle column, rate the quality of sleep you experienced that night, with 1 being excellent and 10 being poor. In the right-hand column, rate your anxiety/ panic from 1 to 10, with 1 being low and 10 intense.

	Sleep Quality	Level of Anxiety/Panic
Day 1 *Number of drinks:* _____ *Time of day:* _____		
Day 2 *Number of drinks:* _____ *Time of day:* _____		
Day 3 *Number of drinks:* _____ *Time of day:* _____		
Day 4 *Number of drinks:* _____ *Time of day:* _____		
Day 5 *Number of drinks:* _____ *Time of day:* _____		
Day 6 *Number of drinks:* _____ *Time of day:* _____		
Day 7 *Number of drinks:* _____ *Time of day:* _____		

The 10 Best-Ever Anxiety Management Techniques Workbook

Break Into Your Cigarette Break

Everyone knows it is a good idea to stop smoking, and anxious smokers know that smoking is hard to give up. When I talk to people with anxiety about why they smoke, especially after they quit and are a bit more honest with themselves, they consistently talk about the cigarette allowing them to get away from anxiety-provoking situations or just take a break that they would not otherwise allow themselves.

Techniques to quit smoking are beyond the scope of this book, but breaking into your cigarette break can help get you on the right path. It's basically about developing ways to get a break that do not require cigarettes, and learning to differentiate nicotine craving from anxiety. Once you can get a break without a smoke, you will be better set up to quit smoking entirely when you decide to take that step.

First, you will need some ideas about how to get a little break, whether at home or work, that are specifically good for you and your setting. List five things you can do for 2 to 5 minutes that feel relaxing. For example:

- Diaphragmatic breathing
- Walking up and down the stairs a few times
- Calling your spouse or partner on the phone
- Looking at pictures of your last vacation
- Stretching

You will use these as a way to get a little break before you smoke. See Figure 3.2.

Break Into Your Cigarette Break

Whenever you feel like you need a cigarette, follow the steps below.

1. Rate your anxiety level from 1 to 10, with 10 being highest: _____
2. Choose an item from your list of relaxing activities and do it.
3. Now, again rate your anxiety level from 1 to 10: _____
4. Now ask yourself, "Do I still want nicotine?" If the answer is yes, then take the cigarette for the nicotine, not for the relaxation break.

Figure 3.2 Break Into Your Cigarette Break

TECHNO STRESS

Technology improves our lives in many ways, but it also contributes to stress. If you aren't a "computer person," new technologies at work may leave you feeling frustrated or confounded, and the consequences of not learning new programs can be severe. Parents who are not comfortable enough with computers or smartphones to monitor and control a child's access to websites can feel intense levels of stress. Even if you do learn new technologies easily, use of them can cut into your time to relax, your ability to sleep, and your sense of connection to other people. There are four common sources of techno stress:

> *Hint: Adolescents do not willingly turn off phones or computers, so parents have to take charge. Confiscate phones during homework or overnight to lower your child's level of technostress. The reduction in anxiety is worth the fight.*

- Email. Before the advent of email, people actually stopped working when they left work. Today, almost everyone who uses email is still taking work-related messages at all times of the day. This interferes with quality sleep and getting other work done.
- Answering calls and texts. The compulsion to answer incoming calls during face-to-face meetings or family activity time (like meals, shopping, or riding together in the car) is very strong. It is sad and ironic that people face-to-face with each other get glued to electronic communication.
- The ubiquitous notification signal. Whether the signal is chiming, dinging, buzzing, beeping, or chirping "You've got mail!" it registers in your brain and your brain keeps you on edge until you check it.
- The sheer volume of information you are expected to respond to. You may experience "data smog"—too much irrelevant data (e.g., receiving unnecessary "reply all" messages)—or "information overload" when sorting through volumes of data to find the pearls you need. The volume takes a toll on your ability to concentrate and remember.

Create Demand Delays

Creating "demand delays" is about (1) assessing your level of techno stress by seeing how anxious it makes you to delay your responses to these demands for attention, and (2) ultimately being in control of *when* you respond to techno demands.

First, make a deliberate choice to limit your availability to answer phone calls, emails, text messages, faxes, pagers, and so on, and see how your anxiety level changes. Following are a few ideas; choose the one that fits best with your work life.

- Wait to check email for at least an hour into your workday. Try getting some work done first.
- Check voicemail, take messages, and return calls at specific times in your day when it suits your schedule best.
- Turn off everything at home that rings or dings, including cell phones, while you eat your meal. Make mealtimes a "no-call zone."
- Turn off your hand-held device during face-to-face meetings, or put notification signals on silent.
- Leave your cell phone in the car when you go into a restaurant, or put it on silent, not vibrate, so that your attention is completely with your meal and your companions. (Do the same thing in movies, theaters, churches, lectures, etc.)
- If you carry a hand-held device especially for work, take it off when you are not on call.
- If you are required to take a computer home or to work from home, make a specific agreement with your supervisor about exactly which hours you are expected to work. Don't respond to messages from work except during those hours.

Once you've selected one of these delays, try it for at least a week. Each day, rate your anxiety level, both during the delay time and after it, on a scale of 1 to 10. At the end of the week, look at the chart to see how your anxiety level changed over the course of the week. You will probably find that as you got more used to doing the delay, your anxiety went down. Figure 3.3 shows a sample chart; use the blank one after that to track your own response to demand delays.

Demand Delay: *Wait 1 hour to do email at work*

Each day, rate your anxiety level, both during the delay time and after it, on a scale of 1 to 10, with 1 being low and 10 being high.

	Anxiety Level During Demand Delay	Anxiety Level After Demand Delay
Day 1	8	2
Day 2	7	3
Day 3	5	2
Day 4	4	1
Day 5	2	1

Figure 3.3 Demand Delay

Demand Delay: _____

Each day, rate your anxiety level, both during the delay time and after it, on a scale of 1 to 10, with 1 being low and 10 being high.

	Anxiety Level During Demand Delay	Anxiety Level After Demand Delay
Day 1		
Day 2		
Day 3		
Day 4		
Day 5		

Notes: _____
_____
_____
_____

As your anxiety levels go down with demand delays, you will become more able to take the breaks you need during the day. When it comes to energy output, people are energetically tuned to sprint and then relax. That is why marathon training is for the few and the hardy! You will function with less anxiety if you take time to recover from the intake of tension generated by too much time with your work technology. Especially for you readers who work at desks with computers, try taking 2 minutes per hour to replenish energy expended throughout the day, and transform a marathon into a series of sprints.

Of course, you may also be using technology compulsively in an effort to take a *break* from work—much like smokers use cigarette breaks to "relax." Responding to every ding and ring from your smartphone or email inbox may be your way of trying to gain relief from the stress of getting a work or school project done. If this is the case, follow the suggestions for taking a break in the section titled "Break Into Your Cigarette Break." Spending a few minutes stretching, looking at pictures, or doing diaphragmatic breathing can be more relaxing than compulsively checking your email.

Track 1 on the CD offers two types of breathing to help you take a short break no matter where you are, the "Balancing Breath" and "Lengthening the Exhale."

QUANTITY OF TECHNO STRESS

The demands of technology may be too much for you to keep up with. When you cannot entirely avoid these technology demands, you must pick a logical way to slow down, control, or interrupt them. Use your demand delays chart to help you decide what arena you want to address first. There are many possibilities, but the categories shown in Figure 3.4 might help you focus on the right next step to alleviate techno stress.

QUALITY OF TECHNO STRESS

Part of reducing techno stress is becoming aware of how it hurts the quality of your life. Many people do not recognize that their time with children or spouses is compromised by emails showing up on a smartphone. They lose out on experiences when they divide their attention, such as answering work emails and texts while watching a child's ballet recital. Constant partial attention to the in-

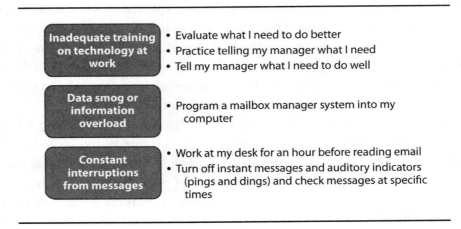

Inadequate training on technology at work	• Evaluate what I need to do better • Practice telling my manager what I need • Tell my manager what I need to do well
Data smog or information overload	• Program a mailbox manager system into my computer
Constant interruptions from messages	• Work at my desk for an hour before reading email • Turn off instant messages and auditory indicators (pings and dings) and check messages at specific times

Figure 3.4 Ideas to Manage Quantity Techno Stress

coming messages distracts your full attention from whatever you are doing, whether you are in a meeting at work, helping a child with homework, or listening to a friend's problem. If you want to improve your memory and concentration, you would do well to reduce the continuous partial-attention energy drain of watching your phone.

For people who work from home, it can be challenging to establish boundaries between personal work and office work. The press of undone work in either arena creates the "never finished" phenomenon. When technology tethers you to it, and you feel the stress of never getting away from it, evaluate what you can turn off and for how long. It will be a relief to stay focused on the people around you at home.

It's also helpful to make clear delineations between work time and home time. One way to do this is to create a specific ritual—even just a short one—to use when you go from work time to home time. You might take a series of deep breaths, change your shoes, or use the Clear the Mind Technique (which is Track 7 on the CD entitled "Contain Your Worry") when you enter your home from your home office. Some other ideas for managing quality techno stress are shown in Figure 3.5.

The 10 Best-Ever Anxiety Management Techniques Workbook

Figure 3.5 Ideas to Manage Quality Techno Stress

PHYSICAL, MENTAL, AND INTERPERSONAL RECOVERY DRILLS

Taking breaks to alleviate stress during work, no matter where you are working, relieves both body and brain. Try the ideas in Figure 3.6 for 2-minute relaxation breaks for physical, mental, and interpersonal recovery. Once you decide which of these ideas works best with your work setting and personal preferences, set up a routine in which you take the 2-minute break every 90 minutes. Set a reminder on your computer or phone so you don't forget.

All of these drills can be adapted for children coming home from school, too. Most school counselors will have ideas about how to give a child some breaks at school during the day, so be sure to consult with the counselor if you think your child could use break time during the school day.

SENSITIVE CHILDREN AND STRESS

Children who have sensitive temperaments and are responsive to noise or confusion, as many children with social anxiety are, need to have ways to calm down or get breaks.

Physical Recovery Drills

Get relief from technology by calming your body.

Breath awareness or diaphragmatic breathing
Hydration (most of us do not drink enough water compared to other beverages)
Exercise ("desk yoga" or taking a 2-minute walk)
Progressive muscle relaxation
Aromas
Healthy snacks, eaten mindfully
Computer-generated biofeedback mechanism (see Appendix for information on devices
  like Heartmath, Stress Eraser, and Wild Divine)

Mental Recovery Drills

Getting away in your mind can be a relief from techno intensity.

Relaxation, meditation, or guided imagery (use earphones to listen if you don't have an
office where you can shut the door)
Music (a listening experience that affects mood and tension levels)
Photos (use digital picture frames or screensavers for visual self-soothing; while looking
  at the photos, contemplate associated memories of people and places)

Interpersonal Recovery Drills

Connecting with others is comforting!

Call a significant other to say hello
Meet a coworker at the water fountain/kitchen for a quick cup of tea
Acknowledge someone who has done a good job or worked hard

Figure 3.6 Physical, Mental, and Interpersonal Recovery Drills

All of these can place demands on sensitive children, tiring them or prompting resistance when there are too many points of stress. Confusion and environmental noise or stimulation can be exhausting. See if there are ways to create quiet zones for your child, like a reading space away from the hubbub. If that's not possible, be sure that there is some time after school for the child to calm down. Use the ideas from the recovery drills in the previous section to create recovery breaks for the child.

S.I.M.P.L.E. PLAN FOR INTERVENING ON INTAKE

This part is simple, but not easy. Start with whichever arena of intake seemed most relevant, whether it is food, alcohol, cigarettes, or technology, and set up a S.I.M.P.L.E. plan to eliminate or replace one of them. It's important to start with just one, because even if you think you should intervene in every arena of intake, doing just one at a time allows you to observe the impact of that specific change and better understand which kind of intake is prompting your anxiety or panic. Changing only one thing at a time will also make you feel less stressed out about change!

It's also important to take care in filling out the "evaluation" part of the chart. Evaluating the results of your changes will strengthen your resolve to continue positive changes in your intake.

Following are a couple of sample S.I.M.P.L.E. charts (Figures 3.7 and 3.8), with a blank one after them for you to fill out.

S.I.M.P.L.E. Plan to Change Intake
(minimizing caffeine intake)

S: What is the *situation* or symptom? *I have a lot of jitteriness and anxious feelings that seem to be worse when I drink caffeine.*

I: What is the *impact* on my life? *It makes it hard for me to feel good, but I drink a lot of coffee to stay alert and I drink diet cola when I am not drinking coffee. I probably drink four cans of cola per day.*

M: What *method* am I trying? *I am going to give up caffeine slowly. I am going to eliminate any caffeine after 3pm. I am going to drink only half-caf coffee and I am going to limit myself to two colas per day. I will do this for a week, then I will go to one cola/day. After 2 weeks, I will drink half-caf coffee only in the morning and none for the rest of the day.*

P: Practice plan. *I am going to have a hard time with the no caffeine after 3 at work. I will try no caffeine in the afternoon on the weekend first and see if there is another beverage I could substitute, like herbal tea or a no-caffeine cold drink.*

L: Lifework. *I will write my goals down and put them someplace where I see them frequently, like on a Post-It stuck to my bathroom mirror or in the Outlook program on my computer.*

E: Evaluate. *I will track my anxiety level at noon and at dinnertime every day for 3 weeks to see if there is an observable impact on my anxiety. I will set my timer in my phone to remind me to check in with myself.*

Figure 3.7 S.I.M.P.L.E. Plan to Change Intake (minimizing caffeine intake)

The 10 Best-Ever Anxiety Management Techniques Workbook

S.I.M.P.L.E. Plan to Change Intake
(separating craving a cigarette from craving a break)

S: What is the *symptom* or *situation*? _I step outside to smoke when I feel anxiety at work._

I: What is the *impact* on my life? _It is inconvenient, especially in bad weather, but it also gives me a really good reason to leave work and be away for a few minutes._

M: What *method* am I trying? _I am going to try stretching in the break room or the bathroom for 2 minutes before I decide to have a cigarette. I am going to rate my anxiety level before I walk away from my workstation and after I stretch._

P: Practice plan. _I can try this out for a week and see if anyone notices what I am doing._

L: Lifework. _I will develop several different methods so that I can have some choices for how to take a break depending on where I am and what the weather is like._

E: Evaluate. _I will note whether I want a cigarette as badly after I stretch. I will evaluate whether I want to decrease cigarette consumption and also whether I smoke less this way._

Figure 3.8 S.I.M.P.L.E. Plan to Change Intake (separating craving a cigarette from craving a break)

S.I.M.P.L.E. Plan to Change Intake

S: What is the *symptom* or *situation?* _____
_____
_____

I: What is the *impact* on my life? _____
_____
_____

```
M:  What method am I trying? _____
_____
_____

P:  Practice plan. _____
_____
_____

L:  Lifework. _____
_____
_____

E:  Evaluate. _____
_____
_____
```

A FINAL WORD

Understanding what aspects of intake are increasing your anxiety level will suggest easy pathways to reduce the physiological symptoms of anxiety. Whether you suffer panic, generalized anxiety, or even social anxiety, relieving sources of agitation and stress may decrease your level of anxiety and prepare you to benefit more from the other techniques in this workbook.

FOUR

Technique #2: Breathe

This technique is the most important one you will ever use to control the physical side of anxiety. It can completely eliminate panic, soothe general anxiety, and keep you calmer when facing social situations so that you can do your best in them.

I find that if people understand why this technique works, they are more willing to try it and more willing to practice. Right now, go ahead and do one simple thing: Take a deep, slow breath, and let it go. Were you aware of your breathing before reading that suggestion? Probably not. Why? It would be impossible to function if you were aware of all your body's automatic functions. We breathe all day without a conscious thought about it. Your body and brain work together to keep you breathing just the right amount, and it never interferes with other things you should be thinking or doing. However, the very moment you decide to breathe, your conscious thought takes over the automatic function of breathing, and you are in control.

> Try it now: Take one deep, slow breath and slowly exhale. You just used the power of your thinking brain to control your automatic brain.

Panic begins with *unconscious activity* in your brain that initiates the sudden rise of heart rate, respiration, and other physical changes that prepare you for fight or flight. The moment you are aware that panic could start or is underway, you can make your breathing conscious and take control of your panic by controlling your breath. You might remember from Chapter 2 that your nervous system cannot be revving up and slowing down at the same time. When you simply start to breathe slowly, the brain-body functions that slow you down take over. Your whole body starts to slow down.

The sensation of generalized anxiety is also caused by unconscious activity. You may feel a sense of dread or impending trouble. You may have tension building even when you are not aware of it until you feel tied in knots. This kind of physical experience of anxiety, which is often accompanied by worrying, causes you to have a physical reaction. Even though it doesn't cause the same dramatic spike in heart rate and respiration as panic, those fight or flight physical responses still kick in, and conscious breathing can be used to calm them.

ASSESS YOUR BREATH

The next time you are under pressure—perhaps during a meeting in which you have to speak or during a disagreement with someone—set aside a part of your attention to observe how your breathing changes when you are tense. It may surprise you to find that you have not been filling your lungs or that you have been holding your breath. Fill out the following chart, putting a check next to all the items that describe your breathing in these stressful situations and adding any other observations you may have.

Assess Your Breath

Type of Breath	✓	Type of Breath	✓
Short or impeded intake *Notes:*		Even, but fast *Notes:*	
Gasping *Notes:*		Relaxed *Notes:*	
Long in, short out *Notes:*		Holding breath *Notes:*	
Shallow *Notes:*		Panting *Notes:*	
Gulping *Notes:*		Hyperventilating *Notes:*	

The 10 Best-Ever Anxiety Management Techniques Workbook

LEARN DIAPHRAGMATIC BREATHING

Taking just one deep breath and letting it go will help relieve some stress, but breathing to control panic works better if you do the method called "diaphragmatic breathing" (Figure 4.1). This is a different type of breath than the short, shallow, panting respirations common to panic. When you breathe in this way you exert control over the pace at which you inhale and exhale.

Practice the first time by lying down or standing—after that, you can breathe anywhere without anyone noticing. Be aware that the goal is not to change the way you breathe as you go about your daily activities but rather to consciously change the way you breathe when you begin to feel panic or anxiety coming on.

Diaphragmatic Breathing

Getting Started

1. Lie down flat on your back or stand in a relaxed manner, feet slightly apart, knees loose. This is so you can sense the movement in your abdomen, which should move out when you inhale and pull in when you exhale.
2. Rest your hand on your abdomen. This will help you to notice if you are breathing deeply enough and whether your chest is tight.
3. Next, exhale the air in your lungs so you are completely empty to start the practice.
4. Now, breathe in through your nose. Inhaling must be done evenly, as if you can fill your lungs from bottom to top in equal, even amounts. One way to imagine this is to think about how a balloon fills with water when you attach it to a faucet. The bottom fills and widens first and then the water expands the upper portion. This image of heaviness as you fill suggests how to imagine your breath. Form an image of your breath filling a balloon in your abdomen, becoming heavy and warm as you inhale.

Finding the Right Pace for You

5. As you inhale, count in your mind as you breathe in. The pace of counting does not matter, as long as you do it at the same pace every time. You might try a pace of one second per count. Count until you feel exactly full (e.g., a slow 1, 2, 3, 4) to help you get a measured, even breath. Chances are you will take between 3 to 6 counts to fill your lungs with smooth inhalations.
6. Then, exhale evenly, taking longer than you did to inhale, at a slow pace until your lungs feel empty. The pace of exhaling should be slow and steady. Imagine you are blowing at the flame of a candle enough to move it but not blow it out. Your body needs time to exchange the oxygen and carbon dioxide or you can get dizzy—a symptom you are trying to eliminate, not encourage!

Figure 4.1 Diaphragmatic Breathing

7. If you are getting dizzy, exhale for two counts longer or pause for two counts at the end of the exhalation of your breath before you start to inhale again.
8. When you find the right pace, write it down. You will use this number to tally practice sessions a bit later. You may find that the pace you like when you are relaxed is different from the pace you like when you are anxious, so make notes about those differences. You may use one pace for breathing to relax and one pace for controlling panic or anxiety.

Figure 4.1 Continued

Make a Record of Your Breathing Pace

Again, the pace you find right for diaphragmatic breathing while relaxed and practicing may be different from the one that works best during stressful situations. Making a record of these differences can be helpful. Figure 4.2 shows a sample record, with one for you to fill out after that.

	My Pace for Breathing When I Am Practicing	My Pace for Breathing When I Am Anxious
Inhale	1, 2, 3, 4, 5	1, 2, 3
Exhale	1, 2, 3, 4, 5, 6, 7	1, 2, 3
Pause	1, 2	1

Figure 4.2 Diaphragmatic Breathing Pace

	My Pace for Breathing When I Am Practicing	My Pace for Breathing When I Am Anxious
Inhale		
Exhale		
Pause		

The main point is taking control of your breath and slowing it. Once you do, you initiate calming throughout your whole nervous system.

Create "Breathing Minutes"

If you want diaphragmatic breathing to work, you will have to master it and then remember to do it! The best way to guarantee that is to practice. You can listen to Track 2, "Diaphragmatic Breathing," on the CD to help you learn and practice breathing. The most effective practice I know involves creating "breathing minutes." For 1 minute at a time, 10 to 15 times a day, practice diaphragmatic breathing. You don't need to be standing or lying down—a good time to practice is whenever you are waiting for something. For example, when you are:

- Stopped at a traffic light
- On hold on the phone
- Waiting in line at a store
- Watching commercials during a television show
- Waiting for the microwave to heat some food
- Waiting for a friend at work or school
- Waiting in the car to pick up someone
- Waiting for the computer to boot
- Waiting for the teacher to hand out the test papers
- Waiting for an instant message or a phone or text message
- Waiting for a meeting to start

Some people prefer to set a timer on their watch, phone, or computer, and when it dings they start breathing for a minute. The more often you practice, the more likely you are to use this technique.

Finally, keeping a tally of the number of breathing minutes you practice each day can help you to establish a good practice schedule. It's easy to do—just carry an index card like that the one shown in Figure 4.3 and mark it whenever you do your 1-minute practice.

My Index Card Record of Breathing Pace and Practice Tally

My pace for breathing when I am practicing: inhale (1, 2, 3, 4, 5) exhale (1, 2, 3, 4, 5, 6, 7) pause (1, 2)

My pace for breathing when I am anxious: inhale (1, 2, 3) exhale (1, 2, 3) pause (1)

My practice tally:
Mon: IIII IIII IIII
Tues: IIII IIII
Wed: IIII IIII IIII I

Figure 4.3 My Index Card Record of Breathing Pace and Practice Tally

Other Good Practice Methods

It is easy to forget to practice, so here are a few more ideas to help you remember:

- Put colored paper dots in odd places—inside a drawer, on the side of the microwave door, on the inside of a car visor, on the cover of a butter dish, or where you can see it when you lift the lid of your copy or scanner machine. Unexpected places are best, where you do not see it all day and begin to ignore it. When you see the dot, stop and breathe for a minute.
  - Program your computer or phone to give you a ding or a pop-up reminder at various intervals during the day.
  - Plan to breathe at specific times every day, such as at the beginning of a class at school or after you brush your teeth.
  - If you like using your hand-held device, there are various "apps" that can remind, guide, and keep track of breathing practice.

> *Hint: Breathe slowly whenever you think of it. You will reduce your overall tension.*

Making Diaphragmatic Breathing Work for a Panic Attack

Controlling panic happens in two ways. One is identifying the signals that you are about to panic. If you start breathing that very second, before the panic starts, you can avert the attack. The other is learning to slow and stop panic when it is underway. After practicing diaphragmatic breathing for 7 days, pick one time of day when you can predict that you will be uninterrupted for a few minutes. For most people it works best to pick early morning, late evening, or your lunch break. During this one uninterrupted period, you are going to add *1 minute of breathing at a time.*

Begin by setting a timer for 2 minutes, and when you can breathe for 2 minutes, set it for 3 minutes the next time. Learn to sustain diaphragmatic breathing for a minimum of 5 minutes. (It's okay if you listen to music while doing this.) You need at least 5 minutes to slow and stop a panic attack that is underway. You may enjoy extending this for 10 minutes. Once you can breathe for this long, you've set the stage to breathe for other important purposes, such as for profound relaxation, meditation, and cueing the stress response to turn itself off.

Obstacles to Diaphragmatic Breathing

Diaphragmatic breathing is a powerful way to disrupt panic and anxiety, but sometimes people have difficulty learning it. Following are a few common obstacles to diaphragmatic breathing, along with ways of getting around them.

- People with breathing problems such as asthma should consider eliminating the counting altogether. For those who do not like the idea of counting, breathe while thinking a sentence with an even rhythm, such as "I am steadily filling my lungs with air. I am emptying my lungs slowly and evenly." Fill up evenly, with no gulps or gasps, so the top is reached physically (in your image of the balloon) just in time to release the breath at the same even, measured pace.
- Some people get anxious when they start to breathe deeply. Some are afraid of their breath because they fear they will panic while doing something new, or the act of breathing reminds them of their panic. Try limiting your breathing to a minute at a time, reminding yourself it is only 1 minute. When that is completely comfortable, add 30-second intervals. If your anxiety continues, you might want to consult a therapist. Anxiety with breathing is sometimes a problem for people who hold their breath to avoid feeling emotions, and you may need support to face that issue.
- It is very rare for diaphragmatic breathing to have no positive impact on panic reduction, but some people report that breathing does not seem to help. Have someone observe how you are breathing, and redo the assessment to see if you are inadvertently resorting to one of those ways of breathing.
- Some people have difficulty concentrating on breathing. The best way to handle this is as follows:
  - Notice that you have been distracted and mentally say to yourself, "Oh. A thought." Just notice, with no judgment against yourself for being distracted. Do not get upset with yourself or impatient with the breathing. Consider thoughts as clouds in the sky, just drifting by. You have no need to stop them, examine them, or be irritated that they are there.

- Redirect your attention to your breath. Focus on the physical sensation of breathing—the feeling of your lungs expanding, the sensation of feeling your waistband or of how your back shifts against a chair, and so on. Feel the breath move through your nostrils or out of your mouth.
- Count to measure the pace to help keep your focus on the breath.

BREATHING FOR MINIMAL AROUSAL

Basic diaphragmatic breathing can help you be calm before any situation that makes you tense. Whether you have generalized anxiety or social anxiety, staying calm or calming down after you get tense starts with breathing. A particularly good 1-minute breathing method to reduce tension involves lengthening your exhale with every breath until you reach the limit of exhaling (Figure 4.4). You can hear this on Track 1 of the CD.

The "5-Count Energizing Breath" method can help you deal with hectic or upsetting situations from which you can take only a short break—such as between classes at school or during a workday. It's especially useful when you need to blow off some steam. You might want to do it privately because it's hard to do subtly—a good place is in the restroom while you're washing your hands. You can do the inhale while washing your hands and then shake water off with five short shakes on the exhale.

Lengthening the Exhale
to Reduce Tension

1. Inhale to the count of 2. Exhale to the count of 2.
2. Inhale to the count of 2. Exhale to the count of 4.
3. Inhale to the count of 2. Exhale to the count of 6.
4. Inhale to the count of 2. Exhale to the count of 8.
5. Inhale to the count of 2. Exhale to the count of 10.

Figure 4.4 Breathing to Reduce Tension

The 5-Count Energizing Breath

1. Inhale to a quick count of 5.
2. Exhale by huffing your breath out in short bursts to the count of 5 (out in bursts: huh-huh-huh-huh-huh).

Figure 4.5 The 5-Count Energizing Breath

S.I.M.P.L.E. PLAN TO PRACTICE BREATHING

Breathing for anxiety management is about as simple as it gets. There is very little to figure out once you can actually do the breath. Just getting yourself to believe it will work is more challenging than actually doing it!

One of the problems with anxiety is that it is consuming and can make remembering what to do to combat it difficult. These breathing techniques are not hard to learn, but you do need to practice them if you want to remember how to do them when you feel anxious. They need to become part of your routine. Look at the sample S.I.M.P.L.E. plan in Figure 4.6 and then create your own.

S.I.M.P.L.E. Plan to Practice Breathing

S: What is the *symptom or situation*? *I have panic attacks that scare me.*

I: What is the *impact on my life*? *I am starting to avoid going into big spaces like malls where I am afraid it will be hard to get out quickly.*

M: What *method* am I trying? *I am going to practice diaphragmatic breathing by slowly breathing and saying to myself, "Now I breathe in all that is of peace; now I breathe out all that is not of peace."*

Figure 4.6 S.I.M.P.L.E. Plan to Practice Breathing

P: Practice plan. _I have set my smartphone alarm to ring three times a day and I will also practice whenever I get into my car._

L: Lifework. _I plan to use this breath when I am in business meetings because the pace and contentiousness are very panic-inducing._

E: Evaluate. _I will wait and observe after 2 weeks if I feel calmer and perhaps have eliminated panic at work._

Figure 4.6 Continued

S.I.M.P.L.E. Plan to Practice Breathing

S: What is the _symptom_ or _situation?_ _____
_____
_____

I: What is the _impact_ on my life? _____
_____
_____

M: What _method_ am I trying? _____
_____
_____

P: _Practice_ plan. _____
_____
_____

L: _Lifework._ _____
_____
_____

E: _Evaluate._ _____
_____
_____

S.I.M.P.L.E. PLAN TO REDUCE TENSION

Breathing is connected to being able to relax your body. People with generalized anxiety often suffer physical tension of many varieties, from jaw tightening to lower back pain. If you have social anxiety, staying calm and collected in situations that might have previously made you tense is an important goal of reducing anxiety. Try breathing when you are tense. Look at the sample S.I.M.P.L.E. plan to reduce tension (Figure 4.7) and then create your own.

S.I.M.P.L.E. Plan to Reduce Tension

S: What is the *symptom* or situation? *Geometry class makes me feel agitated because I don't get it and I am nervous about failing.*

I: What is the *impact* on my life? *I get so worked up that I make stupid mistakes.*

M: What *method* am I trying? *I am going to do the 1-minute breathing techniques when I get into class and whenever I start to feel nervous.*

P: *Practice* plan. *I am going to practice this once every morning to remind myself to do it.*

L: *Lifework. I am going to carry a card that says BREATHE and put it in my geometry book.*

E: *Evaluate. I should be able to tell immediately if I feel better. I will have to wait and see if my grade turns out okay!*

Figure 4.7 S.I.M.P.L.E. Plan to Reduce Tension

S.I.M.P.L.E. Plan to Reduce Tension

S: What is the *symptom* or *situation*? _____
_____
_____

I: What is the *impact* on my life? _____
_____
_____

M: What *method* am I trying? _____
_____
_____

P: *Practice* plan. _____
_____
_____

L: *Lifework.* _____
_____
_____

E: *Evaluate.* _____
_____
_____

A FINAL WORD

Breathing methods are an easy, powerful technique to reduce or eliminate physical symptoms of panic and anxiety. Practice until it comes naturally, and you will master physical anxiety for life.

FIVE

Technique #3: Practice Mindfulness With Shifting Awareness

Anxiety, by nature, is focused on what was or what will be. It is rarely focused on the moment. If something bad is happening *right now*, you are probably not *anxious* or *worried* about it—rather, you are probably dealing with it. Of course, this doesn't mean that whatever is happening isn't scaring you—it very well may be—but there's a difference between actively dealing with a situation while you are scared and being anxious or worried about something in the past or future.

Mindfulness is a way of being fully present in the moment you are living in. Such presence is the antithesis of anxiety. Mindfulness as a practice has recently begun getting well-deserved attention in the world of anxiety management, contributing a great deal even since I wrote *The 10 Best-Ever Anxiety Management Techniques*.

You may have already studied mindful meditation on your own. Applications of mindfulness and meditation are rapidly developing to help people not only with anxiety but also with depression, anger management, and personality disorders, as well as many physical problems, from pain and headaches to cardiovascular problems.

This chapter deals with only one aspect of this practice: mindfulness with shifting awareness. This one exercise can bring immediate benefit to you if you are overfocused on sensations in your body and what they mean, as happens with panic, social anxiety, and generalized anxiety. Over time it will help you ignore fleeting and inconsequential physical sensations.

ASSESS YOUR FOCUS ON BODILY SENSATIONS

People with panic disorder are highly vigilant to the physical signs of panic start-ing—increased heart rate, increased respiration, and so on. People with social anxiety are similarly attuned to physical sensations. When they begin flushing, sweating, or shaking, they worry that other people will see these physical reac-tions and judge them negatively. People with generalized anxiety often plunge into worry by focusing on sensations of dread that are really just the byproduct of brain chemistry. Whenever you focus on such sensations, you doom yourself to having the physical reaction you fear.

Do you overfocus on your bodily sensations? Look at the pattern shown in Figure 5.1 and see if you recognize yourself.

ASSESS WHETHER YOU TALK YOURSELF INTO FEELING FEAR

Do talk yourself into feeling fear? Think back to the last time you had a panic attack or were so embarrassed in a social situation that you had to leave. How did

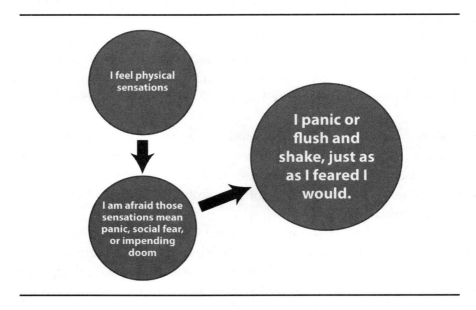

Figure 5.1 Overfocus on Bodily Sensations

The 10 Best-Ever Anxiety Management Techniques Workbook

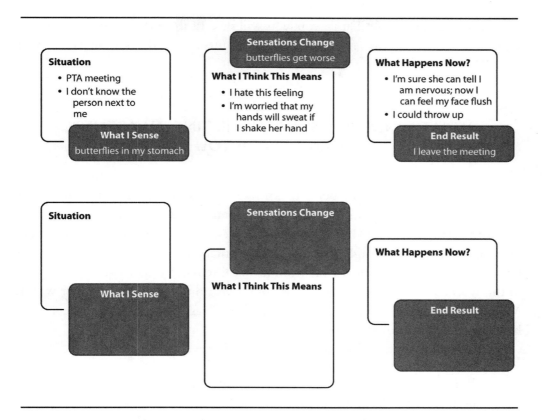

Figure 5.2 *Do You Talk Yourself Into Feeling Fear?*

you feel and what did it mean to you? Describe the situation in the following blank diagram (a sample filled-out diagram precedes it in Figure 5.2).

If you find that you cannot fill this in, don't worry. The next time you get panicky, feel socially anxious, or feel dread that you turn into worry, pay attention. Ask yourself these questions:

- Did I feel the physical sensations (e.g., dread, panic, queasiness) first?
- Did I worry about whether those sensations would get worse?
- Did they get worse?
- Did I then start to really worry, have a panic attack, or get flushed and sweaty?

If this pattern is familiar to you, you will benefit from the mindfulness technique. You can listen to "Mindfulness with Shifting Awareness" on Track 3 of the CD.

WHAT MINDFULNESS WITH SHIFTING AWARENESS CAN DO FOR YOU

Sara, a client of mine, had developed debilitating panic attacks in adulthood. Diaphragmatic breathing helped her know she was not dying while having a panic attack, but she was still afraid of having panic. And she panicked often. She believed every little tingle heralded a panic attack. She created panic out of small, normal changes like a slight chill or a momentary flutter in her stomach. She needed to turn her attention away from physical sensations to what was going on in the world around her—to notice the outer world rather than her inner world. Mindfulness with shifting awareness helped her learn to do that and decreased her panic attacks immediately.

How did it do this? The technique helps in several ways:

- It gives you a sense of control. By focusing attention on what is happening around you, you gain some sense of control over how you are experiencing the moment. You are *choosing* what to attend to.
- It enhances your ability to observe yourself. Our uniquely human capacity to use the brain to control the brain is at the heart of anxiety management, and it is most obvious in selecting what to pay attention to.
- It helps you calm yourself by ignoring disturbing physical sensations. When you intentionally turn your focus from one thing (a physical sensation) to another (observations of the outer world), you calm yourself. This is one method of self-soothing—an important life skill.

MINDFULNESS WITH SHIFTING AWARENESS

The CD provided with this workbook will lead you through this technique. If you prefer not to use the CD, it will be helpful if you do this for the first time

The 10 Best-Ever Anxiety Management Techniques Workbook

with a partner who can read the script below to you. This way you can devote your full attention to your own awareness without being distracted by reading instructions.

The basic steps are as follows:

1. Sit comfortably with your eyes closed.
2. Be aware of the outside world. What do you notice through your senses (ears, nose, skin)?
3. Shift your awareness back to your body. Notice how it feels as you draw breath into your body, as you inhale through your nose. Notice each sensation of inhaling.
4. Notice how it feels to exhale the breath out of your body, exhaling through your nose or mouth. Notice each sensation of exhaling.
5. One more time, shift your awareness to the external world. Be aware of the outside world. What do you notice through your senses?
6. Prepare to open your eyes by becoming aware of light coming through your eyelids, and then gradually allow your eyes to open. Bring your attention to the next activity that you are engaging in.

MAKING IT WORK FOR YOUR TYPE OF ANXIETY

As mentioned earlier, this technique works for panic, social anxiety, and generalized anxiety. Following are a few ideas that might help you make the technique work in various situations and with different types of anxiety.

Mindfulness for Panic Attacks

If you panic, you probably fear having another attack. Mastering this technique will be a big help in getting you to stop:

- Fearing frequent panic attacks
- Fearing "out of the blue" attacks

- Fearing that your panic will worsen if you ignore symptoms of panic
- Fearing new situations in which you might panic

When you have panic disorder, physical sensations may trigger worry that an attack is headed your way. This leads you to escape whatever you are doing at that moment. And when you try to reenter that situation, your brain will watch out for panic. By using this technique to focus on the external world, you can avoid triggering your own panic.

If you have the occasional "out of the blue" attack, use the technique to immediately breathe and shift your focus away from physical sensations. This will ward it off.

If you feel a panic attack coming on before you are fully practiced in breathing or mindfulness, the attack may in fact develop. But don't despair! With practice (and learning the cognitive techniques in Part III), you will eventually get a handle on managing your panic. Until then, remember that you don't need to be afraid of panic happening—it won't last long and although it's unpleasant, it's not lethal.

Mindfulness for Social Anxiety

Let's get this on the table: Other people *do* notice if you are red in the face, sweating, or shaky. But you must know this also: They don't care! (That is, once you are out of junior high school.) The awfulness of social anxiety symptoms depends on what you tell yourself about them.

Cognitive and behavioral techniques (covered in Parts III and IV) are especially effective in managing social anxiety. But warding off the physical symptoms of anxiety that others notice—small signs of flushing, sweating, or shaking—is a critical component of reducing attacks of nervousness. Mindfulness with shifting awareness can take you:

- Inward (staying focused on breathing rather than on the surrounding hubbub can help you avoid the overstimulation that triggers blushing, sweating, or flushing)
- Outward (by not overfocusing on whether you are showing nervousness, you make yourself care about it less, which reduces the likelihood that you will get seriously flushed or shaky)

Symptoms of social anxiety—that embarrassed, flustered look and feeling—are harder to interrupt than panic, in part due to the fact that others *do* notice these symptoms. Ultimately, if you stop caring whether you flush, you diminish your tendency to do so, but the best way to keep these symptoms at bay is to stay calm in situations that could provoke anxiety about being observed. Mindfulness will do that for you.

> *Hint: You can look someone in the face and quietly pay attention to the way your breathing feels. They won't know unless you tell them.*

Mindfulness for Generalized Anxiety

Because this technique can be done in any setting without obviousness—as long as you simply keep your eyes downcast and not closed—it is a terrific tool for pulling the mind away from worry and directing it to the present moment. As mentioned earlier, the antithesis of worry is to be in the moment and not in the future or past. Because generalized worry occurs anywhere for any reason, this "do it anywhere" technique is terrific for those of you who fret.

S.I.M.P.L.E. PLAN FOR PRACTICING MINDFULNESS WITH SHIFTING AWARENESS

Like diaphragmatic breathing, the mindfulness technique requires practice so that it comes easily when you need it most. Your assignment: Print the instructions in Figure 5.3 on an index card, then make a S.I.M.P.L.E. plan to use it, and carry it with you to remind yourself to try it.

Mindfulness with Shifting Awareness

1. Close your eyes and breathe, being fully aware of what your body feels when you breathe.
2. While keeping your eyes closed or downcast, shift your awareness to what you hear, smell, and sense on your skin.
3. Repeat these two steps several times.

Figure 5.3 Mindfulness With Shifting Awareness Instructions

```
┌─────────────────────────────────────────────────────────────┐
│           S.I.M.P.L.E. Plan to Practice Mindfulness           │
│                   With Shifting Awareness                     │
│                                                               │
│  S:  What is the symptom or situation? _____  │
│  _____    │
│  _____    │
│                                                               │
│  I:  What is the impact on my life? _____  │
│  _____    │
│  _____    │
│                                                               │
│  M:  What method am I trying? _____  │
│  _____    │
│  _____    │
│                                                               │
│  P:  Practice plan. _____  │
│  _____    │
│  _____    │
│                                                               │
│  L:  Lifework. _____  │
│  _____    │
│  _____    │
│                                                               │
│  E:  Evaluate. _____  │
│  _____    │
│  _____    │
└─────────────────────────────────────────────────────────────┘
```

A FINAL WORD

This simple technique is a gem for all types of anxiety, and it comes with the added benefit of being very relaxing.

SIX

Technique #4: Relax

Rest and relaxation are not necessarily the same, but lack of rest makes it hard to be relaxed, and sleeping is difficult if you are not relaxed. A great benefit of knowing how to relax is improvement in quality of sleep. If you suffer any type of anxiety, you are experiencing physical signs of that negative physical arousal. People with panic have to deal not only with the attack itself but also with its aftermath, and it may take a long time to calm down. Learning to relax intentionally can help with the discomfort of a panic attack and its aftermath. People with generalized anxiety are likely to be physically tense as well as emotionally uptight. They may have physical conditions that are made worse by tension: headaches, TMJ, digestive problems, and so on. Developing a habit of relaxation practices will help diminish that tension. Those with social anxiety may feel comfortable when there is no risk of being observed, but trying to stay calm while imagining an upcoming distressing situation (like speaking in public) poses a different kind of relaxation problem. Taking charge of the physical experience of anxiety by intentionally relaxing the body helps with those situations as well.

Physical relaxation does not come naturally to people suffering anxiety. People with generalized anxiety—the worriers and high-drive people—show tension-related arousal, and they may not notice how they have tightened up in the neck or shoulders, lower back, buttocks, or legs until they have pain somewhere. Tension headaches are born of tense muscles in the head and neck that restrict blood flow or affect nerves. For people who suffer panic attacks, the mental tension of expecting an attack and watching for signs of it leads to ten-

Figure 6.1 Physical Tension Increases Likelihood of Anxiety Attacks

sion in the body. For those with social anxiety, the tension prior to being in a public situation in which they fear they are going to be humiliated can be intense. It causes them to tighten up and be more subject to panic or social anxiety symptoms. Figure 6.1 shows this vicious cycle.

ASSESS YOUR NEED TO RELAX

Every kind of anxiety is stressful. Knowing you might panic or feel intense social anxiety raises the stress level of your social encounters; being in public settings or doing activities you fear could trigger your symptoms. Stress from work raises anxiety levels. Regardless of the source of your anxiety, your body reacts. You produce more adrenaline and cortisol, and have increased heart rate, blood pressure, and muscle tension. Digestive processes change: You may feel nausea, have increased urgency of urination, or have diarrhea.

Each of the three major types of anxiety addressed in this workbook—panic, generalized anxiety, and social anxiety—has hallmark signs of tension or physical arousal. Check the following lists to see what physical indicators you have. If you suffer from more than one kind of anxiety, you may check symptoms in two or all three categories.

Do You Have These Symptoms?

Do you have any of the following symptoms of panic:

- ☐ Rapid heart rate
- ☐ Shallow breathing
- ☐ Digestive upset
- ☐ Sweating
- ☐ Shakiness, trembling
- ☐ Dizziness
- ☐ Exhaustion when the attack subsides
- ☐ Feelings of tingling, agitation long after the attack subsides

Do you have any of the following symptoms of generalized anxiety:

- ☐ Abdominal pain (this symptom of anxiety is one reported by children)
- ☐ Chest pain
- ☐ Dry mouth or difficulty swallowing
- ☐ Headaches
- ☐ Muscle tension (neck, upper back, lower back)
- ☐ Holding your breath
- ☐ Muscle weakness
- ☐ Fatigue
- ☐ Trouble concentrating
- ☐ Restless sleep

Do you have any of the following symptoms of social anxiety:

- ☐ Blushing
- ☐ Sweating
- ☐ Heart palpitations
- ☐ Shaking hands or knees
- ☐ Quivering voice
- ☐ Nausea

All of these symptoms are related to your body being in a state of arousal. Relaxation, done deliberately, can avert or alleviate these symptoms.

TENSE-AND-RELEASE PROGRESSIVE MUSCLE RELAXATION

Progressive muscle relaxation for tension release is a "first line" treatment for the physical tension of the anxious body. When combined with slow, deep breathing, this intentional relaxation of muscles helps the parasympathetic nervous system lower blood pressure and slow heart rate and respiration. This technique not only eliminates tension-related stiffness and aches but also lowers arousal levels, which makes triggering anxious physical symptoms more difficult.

The tense-and-release progressive muscle relaxation is provided on Track 9 of the CD that accompanies this workbook. If you'd rather not use a CD, you can follow the steps below.

The muscle relaxation will take 10 to 15 minutes. The basic gist of it is to relax all muscle groups in a systematic manner, as follows:

1. Tighten and then release each muscle group—slowly progressing from head to toe—three times before going to the next muscle group.
2. Follow this order: head, neck, shoulders, arms, hands/fingers, chest, abdomen, hips, thighs, shins/calves, ankles, feet/toes.
3. Before moving from one group to the next, feel warmth flood into that muscle group.
4. End with feeling how your feet are connected to the ground.

Muscle Relaxation With Children and Elderly Adults

Because this technique can be done seated or lying down, there is no reason that older adults can't do it. If tensing muscles feels uncomfortable, however, you can substitute stretching in place of it. Stretching follows the same procedure as tense-and-release relaxation, but uses stretching instead of tightening. It is the preferable method for people with sore muscles, arthritis, or connective tissue disorders. As with all exercises, follow the common sense rule: Never do anything that hurts! Sometimes stretching out tense muscles can feel a bit achy, but it should be more like a "good soreness" than outright pain.

Children may not suffer the same muscle tension from anxiety, but they do experience problems with digestion. Relaxation training can help with that. Doing a physical relaxation is especially useful when children do not cognitively recognize their stress or anxiety. Depending on the child's age, you can improve attention and cooperation by making stretching and relaxing into a game. It can be fun for smaller children to stretch out using images of animals they can relate to (e.g., "stretch your arms and back like a cat stretching out in the sun" or "stretch your face like a lion opening its mouth to yawn"). In a classroom setting, stretching as a group exercise can help children and adolescents relax before things that would make anyone uptight, like taking a test. By having the whole classroom participate, you don't single out any one child, decreasing his or her anxiety about being noticed.

SPHERE OF LIGHT IMAGERY FOR RELAXATION

Imagery for muscle relaxation works very well for many, and you can do it even if you have physical restrictions. It requires less time than tense-and-release progressive muscle relaxation. This "sphere of light" technique works to relax your whole body, and it is great for people who enjoy imagery. You can use the CD or follow the steps below. Following is a brief description of the technique:

1. Imagine a glowing sphere of light above your head. Vibrant with warmth and energy, it is the color you associate with peace or calm.
2. Inhale the light through the top of your head.
3. Exhale the warmth of the light down through your body, from the top of your head through every part until you reach your feet.
4. Notice the progress of warm, vibrant energy through each muscle group.
5. Associate a particular word with this sensation, and if you feel tense at any time later in the day, just take a breath, say the word, remember the sensation, and become immediately relaxed.

ONE-BREATH (OR "CUED") MUSCLE RELAXATION

Once you have learned diaphragmatic breathing and progressive muscle relaxation, you can pair them to produce "cued relaxation." This is a way to relax

---

Creating Cued Relaxation

Use the following steps to pair diaphragmatic breathing with muscle relaxation.

1. Several times a day, take a deep, diaphragmatic breath, recalling the way you feel when you are deeply relaxed.
2. Use an image that represents letting tension go—such as plugging your feet into the earth—and as you exhale, send negative energy out of your body and let relaxation flow in behind it throughout the whole body. (Another good image is to send roots from your feet into the earth to draw calm in, and send tension off into the atmosphere.)
3. Accompany a slow, deep breath in with a calming statement, such as "Now I am breathing in all that is of peace. Now I am breathing out all that is not of peace." Whether using an image or a phrase, draw peaceful relaxation inward as you inhale, and exhale the negative energy.
4. When you exhale, send the energy off or out in the way you have imagined it. Note how the muscles from your scalp to your toes let go of tension. Repeat this many times a day.

Figure 6.2 Creating Cued Relaxation

physically and mentally with one breath. Doing it several times every day can greatly reduce the impact of muscle tension. It also helps you when you sense you are about to panic or when you are in situations that make you tense. If you have social anxiety and are in a situation that raises your tension, this is a subtle way to calm down.

As you get comfortable with this pairing, you will be able to take one breath and feel all your muscles release. In this way you *cue* muscle relaxation on demand—anywhere, anytime—without anyone noticing.

S.I.M.P.L.E. PLAN FOR MUSCLE RELAXATION

Create a S.I.M.P.L.E. plan for muscle relaxation so you can hold yourself accountable for learning it. Figure 6.3 shows a sample S.I.M.P.L.E. plan; a blank one appears after that for you to fill out.

S.I.M.P.L.E. Plan for Muscle Relaxation

S: What is the *situation* or *symptom*? *I am tense at work, especially when sitting at the computer all day. I tend to clench my teeth while I work, worrying about my job.*

I: What is the *impact* on my life? *I have headaches from this and my neck gets tight.*

M: What *method* am I trying? *I will do daily cued relaxation at least 5 times per workday.*

P: Practice plan. *I will make sure I know diaphragmatic breathing and progressive muscle relaxation. I have done them before, but I will try them several times to be sure I remember them correctly.*

L: Lifework. *I will set my task manager to cue me once per hour to do cued relaxation.*

E: Evaluate. *I will notice in 1 week if I feel less neck tension or have fewer headaches.*

Figure 6.3 S.I.M.P.L.E. Plan for Muscle Relaxation

S.I.M.P.L.E. Plan for Muscle Relaxation

S: What is the *symptom* or *situation?* _____
_____
_____

I: What is the *impact* on my life? _____
_____
_____

M: What *method* am I trying? _____
_____
_____

P: *Practice* plan. _____

_____

_____

L: *Lifework.* _____

_____

_____

E: *Evaluate.* _____

_____

_____

EXERCISE TO RELAX

You don't have to sit still to relieve your anxiety and tension. In fact, movement may be exactly what you need.

A stunning amount of research demonstrates the many ways exercise is good for your mind and body. For the high-energy person with lots of muscle tension, physical activities are a better way of relaxing than sitting still is, but exercise can help people with *all* kinds of anxiety. Exercise:

- Promotes healthy brain activity by increasing blood flow
- Keeps the body healthy and able to respond effectively to stress
- Improves self-efficacy—a feeling often diminished when feeling stress

This section will help you get started on exercise. See the Recommended Reading & Resources for resources to consult for more information.

Getting Started

Of all forms of exercise, aerobic exercise is best for anxiety because it is both a long-term relaxer and a short-term tension-releaser. But if you don't yet have an exercise routine, starting at that pace may be too difficult. It is fine to build slowly, doing things you might actually enjoy, so that you have a good chance of staying with it.

The biggest problem may be getting started, so starting small is best. Make a commitment to do one or two small exercise increases. You might begin by committing to walk the dog for an extra block or 5 extra minutes, or by getting off the bus one stop before you have to, or by walking around the block once whenever you check the mail. It is important to specifically decide on a small

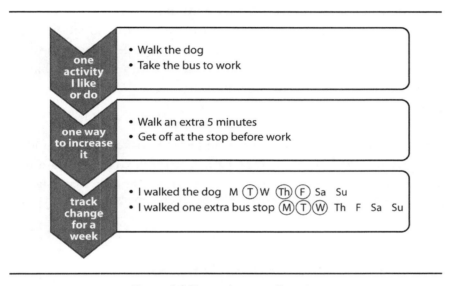

Figure 6.4 Plan to Increase Exercise

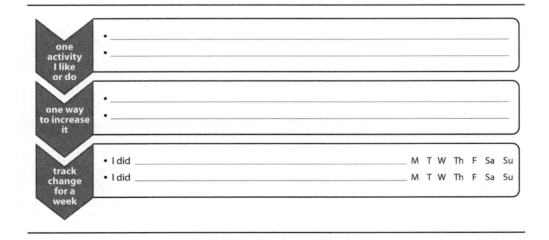

step and make a commitment to do it. Figure 6.4 shows an example of a plan to increase exercise; a blank one for you to fill out is offered after it.

If you want to build up to 25–45 minutes of aerobic activity, start by asking yourself these questions:

1. What physical things do I like to do?
2. What are my opportunities to do it?
3. Is there anyone who would do it with me?
4. What is the largest possible step I can take in the direction of exercise? (Your weekly goal should be to do a little more each week, until you have achieved the goal of 25–45 minutes of aerobic exercise at 70% of your maximum heart rate.)
5. How will I be accountable?

One way to be accountable is to use a simple record-keeping method like the one in Figure 6.5. You can draw the chart on an index card and use it to help you keep track. This is another arena where "apps" for your hand-held device have good tracking options.

STRETCH TO RELAX

Stretching is useful because you can do it anywhere, anytime (Figure 6.6). Several of these stretches can be done while you're at work or school or sitting in

	Day 1	Day 2	Day 3	Day 4	Day 5	Day 6	Day 7
Type of exercise: _____ Duration: _____							
Type of exercise: _____ Duration: _____							

Figure 6.5 Exercise Record

Quick Stretches That Can Be Done Anywhere

- *Yawn-and-stretch.* Simply yawn, stretch your arms upward, and release. Repeat.

- *Torso relaxation.* For gentle back stretching, try torso relaxation. Standing with your feet comfortably spread apart for support, let your head fall forward, leading the torso down and bending at the waist. Return to an upright position by reversing the motion. Continue the action of this simple stretch into an overhead stretch once you are upright. Lift up your arms, reaching high overhead, and gently tilt your head by lifting your chin until you gaze directly up. Make this and all releases gentle.

- *Leg lunges.* If you get up to walk somewhere, pause for a moment and do gentle leg lunges. This is great when you have been sitting too long or are too tight.

- *Calf stretch.* If you have the opportunity to go up or down a few stairs, pause, hold the handrail, and with your toes balanced on the edge of the stair, let your heel drop, thereby stretching the back of your leg. Do this for 2 seconds of stretch and then pause. Repeat it a few times. You can do this one leg at a time with the other foot firmly planted on the stair so you don't have to worry about balance.

- *Head tilt.* Tilt your head so that your ear falls toward your shoulder as far as it can without hurting. Then raise your head upright. Let your chin drop slowly to your chest, feel the stretch down your back, and then raise your head upright. Drop the other ear toward your shoulder and, again, raise your head upright. Let your head feel heavy and drop slowly backward. Return to an upright position before you repeat this. *Do not rotate your neck in a circle.* You can do this while seated at your desk, even as you talk on the phone or look at the computer, without losing any time from work.

- *Arm stretch.* Raise one arm straight overhead and then bend it at the elbow, reaching with that hand down as if you were going to scratch between your shoulder blades.

Figure 6.6 Quick Stretches That Can Be Done Anywhere

Then relax. With the same arm, reach across your chest and wrap your hand around the opposite shoulder. Using the unoccupied hand, grasp the elbow of the reaching arm and gently exert pressure to increase the stretch in the shoulder and upper arm. Again, you can do this while seated at your desk without interrupting work time.

- *Seated posture change.* You can prevent the tightening up that occurs when seated at a desk using the seated posture change. This preventive measure can be practiced constantly if your job requires sitting all day. It involves regularly rotating through changed positions. Have a small stool (or just a box) by your feet on which to rest them. In the first position, sit with one foot raised. In the next, sit with the other foot raised. Then sit with both raised, and then neither. Hold each position for 15 minutes before rotating to the next. Another version of this exercise is to use a back pillow or rolled towel, and put it first behind your lower back, then your middle back, and then do without it.

Figure 6.6 Continued

any confined place such as a car or airplane seat. They take no time to speak of, requiring you only to pause in whatever activity you are doing. You can stretch while thinking about the next question on a test, while you wait on hold on a phone call, or as your computer prints a document. Although one 15-second stretch is sufficient to release a little tension, some stretching experts recommend several 2-second stretches to loosen up, so do what feels best to you. Practicing these stretches will help keep you loose when things could make you uptight.

SLOW DOWN TO RELAX

Some people find it very challenging to start an exercise routine. All is not lost. There are other ways to diminish the impact of stress and relax tension. You may feel anxious about doing the relaxing activities in Figure 6.7, thinking you're being lazy or unproductive, but just remember this: Tension and anxiety take a toll on your productiveness as well, and you'll be more efficient and (happier) if you are relaxed while you work.

Relaxing Activities

- *Massage.* There are many different types of massage, but even the simplest neck massage from a family member reduces the impact of stress.
- *Warm bath with aromatherapy.* Aromatherapy is the practice of using essential oils to enhance relaxation and target symptoms of tension and anxiety. The oils are highly concentrated substances distilled from plants known to have therapeutic benefit. You can use the scent in bath or deliver it via other methods.
- *Stroll in the sun.* Just 30 minutes of walking outside provides enough light stimulation to help you stay more energized in gray weather. Being in the warmth of the sun is also a good muscle relaxer.
- *Time near lapping or running water.* Whether it's a lake, a river, or an ocean, the sounds are soothing. Breathe as you listen to them. Time in the natural world brings many benefits of relaxation.

Figure 6.7 Relaxing Activities

Your assignment: Slow down by deciding to do one of these relaxing activities and committing to it.

"I will make a commitment to do _____ by this date _____."

SLEEP!

It's impossible to be relaxed when you're exhausted. Good sleep underlies good health, including good mental health. When a person has anxiety, sleep suffers for several reasons, depending on the cause of the anxiety. The profound mental relaxation promoted by good rest is not obtainable in any other way. Getting a good night's sleep can often be achieved just by relaxing your body well enough and having the right environment. (Adding the method Clearing the Mind from Chapter 9 can also help. It's called "Contain Your Worry" on Track 7 of the CD.) If that doesn't work, you may need to give your sleep more attention. Check out the section on sleeping in *The 10 Best-Ever Anxiety Management Techniques* for ideas to handle worry dreams, or go to the Recommended Reading and Resources section of this book for heavy-duty sleep management help. Figure 6.8 gives some suggestions for improving your sleep hygiene.

Improving Your Sleep

Set a pattern of sufficient sleep
- Be regular about the times you sleep.
- Make enough time for sleep. Go to bed early enough to stay in bed for a full 8 hours, even if you wake sooner than that for a while.

Make the environment conducive to sleep
- Sleep in a room that is as cool and as dark as possible.
- Screen out environmental noises (like people talking in another room or noise from the street). When the environment has variable noises, like an apartment building, use some form of consistent noise like a fan or white-noise machine.

Prepare the brain and body for sleep
- Eliminate violent or exciting TV for several hours before sleep.
- Take a warm bath for 20 minutes before sleep.
- Create a drowsy brain with herbal teas such as catnip or chamomile.
- Keep caffeine as low as possible, especially after noon, because it is a stimulant.
- Do not work on email, messages, voicemails, or computer projects close to bedtime. A mind racing with ideas will have trouble dropping off to sleep.

Plan to handle restless sleep quality
- Handle worry dreams by awakening fully for a few minutes and shake the dream off by consciously finishing the topic, dispelling its importance, and then focus on something pleasant while falling back to sleep.
- Plan for awake times—literally, plan what you will watch, read, or think about if you awaken to avoid slipping into negativity or worry.

Figure 6.8 Improving Your Sleep

S.I.M.P.L.E. PLAN TO GET STARTED ON RELAXATION

You may want to try all of the relaxation methods suggested in this chapter, or just choose the one or two that appeal to you. Maybe your issue is sleep—not sleeping enough or sleeping too restlessly. Maybe it is just muscle tension that bothers you. Perhaps you want to be more relaxed in meetings or classrooms. Knowing your relaxation goals will help you decide where to start in addressing your particular problem. Figure 6.9 provides a quick look at where to start.

Once you've picked a place to start, fill out a S.I.M.P.L.E. plan to help you

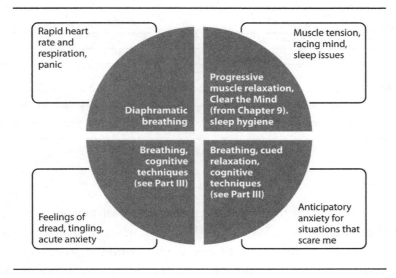

Figure 6.9 Choosing Where to Start

follow through on it. You can certainly try more than one method—if you do, photocopy the following blank S.I.M.P.L.E. plan and fill out a copy for each method.

S.I.M.P.L.E. Plan to Enhance Relaxation

S: What is the *symptom* or *situation*? _____
_____
_____

I: What is the *impact* on my life? _____
_____
_____

M: What *method* am I trying? _____
_____
_____

P: *Practice* plan. _____
_____
_____

L: *Lifework.* _____
_____
_____

E: *Evaluate.* _____
_____
_____

A FINAL WORD

The biggest impediment to using this technique is not believing that relaxation is powerful enough to help when you feel very upset. That may be true when you first start tackling your anxiety, but as you continue to practice this technique, its value will grow. The more you learn to relax your body, the greater the benefit will be to you.

PART III

Managing the Anxious Mind

SEVEN

Technique #5: Stop Catastrophizing

Thoughts that begin with the words "Oh no!" are likely to be followed by thoughts that are "catastrophizing"—that is, thoughts that make the worst of whatever you are about to experience. When you catastrophize, you make a mountain out of a molehill, expecting things to be "awful" or "terrible" or "the worst possible outcome."

Catastrophizing is common in all three types of anxiety—panic, social anxiety, and generalized anxiety. People who suffer panic or social anxiety tend to catastrophize both their symptoms and the outcome of their symptoms. They live in fear of having the strong negative feelings of a panic attack or of the possibility that they will blush, sweat, or shake in a social situation. People who have panic attacks often believe they are dying, going crazy, or losing control. And people with social anxiety are convinced that they will certainly be rejected or feel humiliated and see this as the worst possible feeling they could ever imagine.

When people with generalized anxiety feel that familiar sensation of dread coming on, they go on "scan mode" to see what could be causing it, usually assuming the sensation is due to more than just a glitch in their anxious brain. They will find something wrong in their life to explain the dread, which makes them feel even worse because now they believe, "Yes! Something *is* wrong." Figure 7.1 shows an example of how this can happen.

When you suffer from anxiety, your body—for no good reason other than neurochemistry—generates sensations that feel like anxiety. And the emotional part of your brain, geared to protect you against bad things happening, reacts to these physical signals *as if they are the truth*. Convinced that if you're feeling

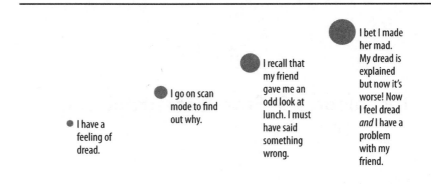

Figure 7.1 Going on Scan Mode to "Catastrophize" Dread Sensation

physical symptoms of anxiety there must indeed be something very real to worry about, the emotional part of your brain catastrophizes the sensations. And it's hard to disbelieve your own brain telling you something bad is about to happen! That's why you need to make deliberate decisions to identify and divert those thoughts.

ASSESS YOUR CATASTROPHIZING

If you catastrophize, you will see yourself in one of the following examples. Figure 7.2 illustrates an example of catastrophizing in panic disorder, Figure 7.3 shows it with social anxiety, and Figure 7.4 shows it with generalized anxiety. Following each of these figures are blanks ones where you can write in your own physical symptoms and the thought process that follows them.

If you see yourself in any of these three examples, read on to learn how to interrupt and defeat catastrophic thinking.

LOGIC VERSUS EMOTION

It's true that the physical symptoms of anxiety are highly unpleasant—so unpleasant, in fact, that when they appear, the emotional part of your brain assumes a catastrophe must be happening:

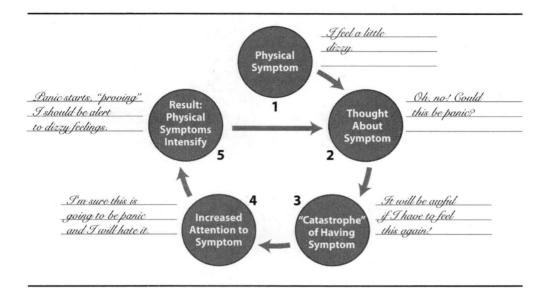

The diagram shows the following labeled cycle:

- **Physical Symptom** (1) — *I feel a little dizzy.*
- **Thought About Symptom** (2) — *Oh, no! Could this be panic?*
- **"Catastrophe" of Having Symptom** (3) — *It will be awful if I have to feel this again!*
- **Increased Attention to Symptom** (4) — *I'm sure this is going to be panic and I will hate it.*
- **Result: Physical Symptoms Intensify** (5) — *Panic starts, "proving" I should be alert to dizzy feelings.*

Figure 7.2 Panic Disorder Catastrophizing

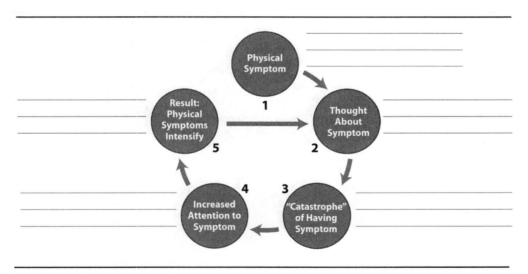

- If you panic fairly often, your brain is sensitized and primed for the next attack. You may believe that you can't control your panic and become terrified when you even *think* about panicking.
- If you have generalized anxiety, your brain goes into "oh, no!" mode when some situation sparks a worry. This triggers a stab of

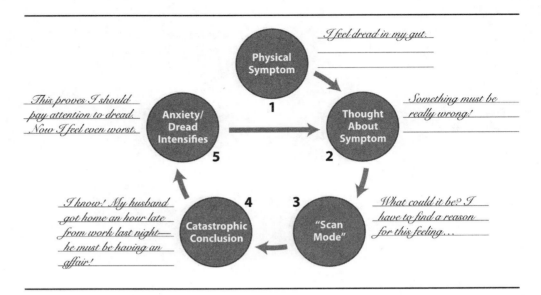

I feel dread in my gut.

Something must be really wrong!

What could it be? I have to find a reason for this feeling...

I know! My husband got home an hour late from work last night—he must be having an affair!

This proves I should pay attention to dread. Now I feel even worst.

Figure 7.3 Generalized Anxiety Catastrophizing

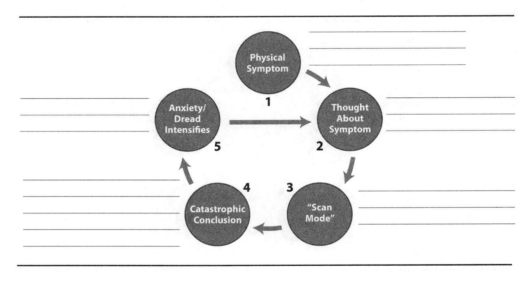

adrenalin, which causes the sensation of stomach-sinking fear. So even if the initial mistake or problem that caused the worry is minor, your skyrocketing anxiety about it makes you believe it's a catastrophe that may not have a reasonable solution.

The 10 Best-Ever Anxiety Management Techniques Workbook

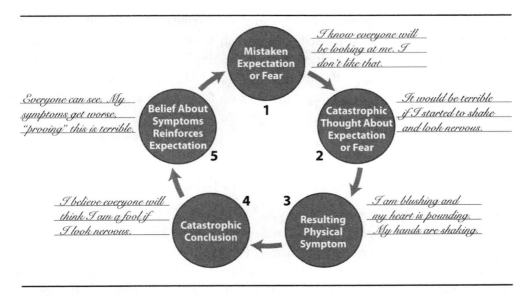

I know everyone will be looking at me. I don't like that.

It would be terrible if I started to shake and look nervous.

I am blushing and my heart is pounding. My hands are shaking.

I believe everyone will think I am a fool if I look nervous.

Everyone can see. My symptoms get worse, "proving" this is terrible.

Figure 7.4 Social Anxiety Catastrophizing

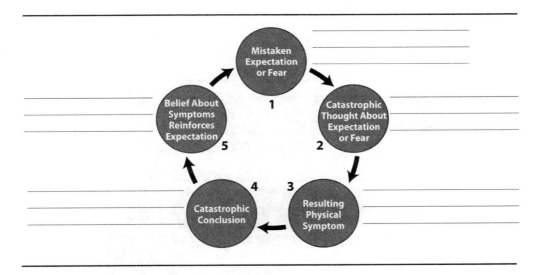

- If you are burdened with social anxiety, you have a brain structure that is more sensitive to feelings of anxiety—those sensations feel worse to you than they feel to other people. You are also overly alert to negative faces, seeing more rejection than is really there.

To defeat catastrophic thinking, you must use deliberate, emphatic logic to override that emotional voice telling you your symptoms are awful or a sign of something bad. In other words, you must use the logical part of your brain to override the emotional part your brain—to say, "Hey, wait! I know you think something very bad is happening, but let's stop for a second to see if that's really true." The following methods will help you do just that.

LEARN THAT A FEELING IS JUST A FEELING

There is a four-step process to help you learn that a feeling is just a feeling and interfere with catastrophic thinking no matter which kind of symptom you're experiencing. This process is described in Figure 7.5.

At the end of this section, there is a blank version of this figure that will help you tailor this four-step process to your own specific symptoms. Before you fill it out, look at the following material on how this technique applies to the three main types of anxiety.

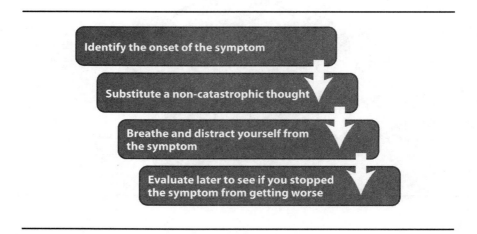

Figure 7.5 Learn That a Feeling Is Just a Feeling

The 10 Best-Ever Anxiety Management Techniques Workbook

Panic Is Unpleasant But Not Lethal

Are the physical symptoms of panic unpleasant? Absolutely. Unwelcome? Yes. Distracting? No doubt. But they are nothing more than that! *They won't kill you.* They are just sensations. Ask yourself: "Have I survived every panic attack?" (If you are reading this, the only answer is "yes"!)

If you suffer from panic, here are some guidelines for filling out the blank "a feeling is just a feeling" diagram.

1. Identify the symptom that gets you on the catastrophic thinking track.
2. Write down the catastrophic thoughts you most often have and substitute them with the corrective thought. For example, you might substitute "if I panic it will be awful" with "panic is unpleasant—but it isn't lethal."
3. Select which breathing method you prefer (see Chapter 4) and a method to distract yourself. For example, you might decide to look at pictures of your last vacation or pat your dog for a minute.
4. Evaluate how this worked. This step helps your brain fight the catastrophic thinking next time.

Coming to believe that "a feeling is just a feeling" requires paying attention to outcomes. Even a full-fledged, extremely unpleasant panic attack is eventually going to stop and leave you unharmed. Noticing the outcome—that an attack was brief and you survived it—and noticing that you suffer less when you do not catastrophize are vital to increasing your confidence that you can stop panic.

Dread Is Just a Feeling That Can Occur Even When Nothing Is Wrong

When else is a feeling just a feeling? High-drive people with generalized anxiety are biologically set up to get a gut feeling that is a lot like the feeling you get when something is about to go wrong—that "uh, oh" feeling of dread. That queasy gut is a signal to look out for something, but it is not an *urgent* feeling, like danger.

To escape catastrophizing, you must believe this: That feeling does not mean anything. Many people want to believe the dread *must* mean something and fight against distracting themselves from it. They ask, "But what if something really is wrong and I ignore it?" The trick is to ask yourself if the dread *preceded* your awareness that something might be wrong. If the answer is "Yes, I noticed the dread first, and then tried to figure it out," you can reasonably assume that there's no good reason for your feelings of worry, and you can proceed to distract yourself from that miserable feeling without figuring it out. (For a longer discussion of the biological basis of dread and some caveats to knowing it is just a feeling without meaning, see my books *The Anxious Brain* and *The 10 Best-Ever Anxiety Management Techniques*.)

If you suffer from generalized anxiety, here are some guidelines for filling out the blank "a feeling is just a feeling" diagram at the end of this section.

1. You get the "uh, oh" feeling of dread—how do you feel it in your body?
2. Stop catastrophizing about this feeling. Substitute a statement such as "dread is just a feeling that can occur even when nothing is wrong" or "if I really have a problem, I won't have to go looking for it."
3. Choose a breathing technique that you like (see Chapter 4), and immediately distract yourself, perhaps by one of the thought replacements in Chapter 8, such as thinking about the work you are doing right at this moment.
4. Evaluate later, noticing that the feeling went away and there was no problem causing it.

Embarrassment Is Just a Feeling

The flushing, trembling, sweaty feelings that seem to happen whenever you are in public are very hard to control. To stop catastrophizing about those feelings, you must do two things: first, dispute what you believe will happen if others notice your nervousness, and then ignore your sensations.

It is true that your signs of anxiety are visible to others. What is *not true* is that others will reject you because you look nervous. Dispute your belief that you will be humiliated or rejected by telling yourself: "Being noticed is not the same thing as being rejected." (Interactions between adolescents are an exception to this. Teenagers are often unkind to each other, and they may indeed make a big deal out of you flushing or sweating. If you are an adolescent, the key to stopping catastrophizing is learning to shrug off the appearance of anxiety. Learning, practicing, and using words and actions that show you are unconcerned—like laughing with peers about your tendency to blush—is a good way to deal with the runaway thoughts of social anxiety. If you need help finding good ways to shrug off the symptoms, ask a parent, trusted teacher, or school therapist.)

Once you have disputed your assumptions about what will happen, it becomes much easier to simply ignore your flushing, shaking, or sweating. You can decide it is *not awful* if that should happen, and just live with it, using breathing to stay as calm as possible.

If you suffer from social anxiety, here are some guidelines for filling out the blank "a feeling is just a feeling" diagram.

1. What are your signs of embarrassment? For example, do you get red in the face, feel a bit nauseous, or find that your voice quivers?
2. Stop catastrophizing about this feeling. Note what you normally say to yourself—such as "it will be awful if they notice I'm sweating"—and substitute that statement with "being noticed is not the same as being rejected."
3. Choose a breathing technique that you like (see Chapter 4), and immediately distract yourself, perhaps by noticing all the decorations in the room.
4. Evaluate later: Did your feeling subside? Were you indeed rejected? Did you have some success in doing some of the social activity without symptoms?

Here is the blank "a feeling is just a feeling" diagram for you to fill out.

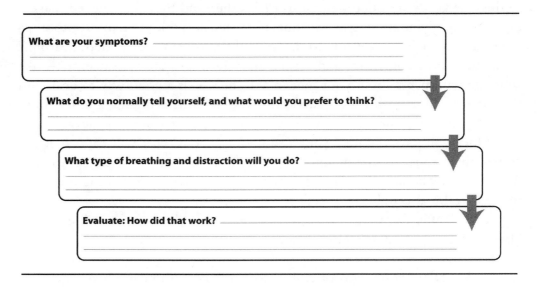

What are your symptoms? _____

What do you normally tell yourself, and what would you prefer to think? _____

What type of breathing and distraction will you do? _____

Evaluate: How did that work? _____

DEBUNK THOUGHTS ABOUT DYING, GOING CRAZY, OR LOSING CONTROL

This method works especially well with panic, although it can be adapted to deal with other types of anxiety as well. People who suffer from panic are especially prone to catastrophize because the sensations are so intense. "I'm dying!" "I'm going crazy!" "I'm losing control!" Although the logical part of your brain knows that you have survived other panic attacks without these consequences, your emotional brain still goes there. And the strength of its belief is powerful: I once had a client who had a panic attack relapse after many months of getting better at preventing them. Even though his logical brain was saying, "It's probably just panic," his emotional brain told him, "But *this* time it could be a heart attack." It was only after a visit to the emergency room and thousands of dollars of medical tests that his emotional brain finally believed his logical brain.

The following two steps will help you override your emotional brain:

1. Tell yourself you have always survived panic.
2. Watch how breathing slows you down, and remind yourself that you know how to stop panic, even when it is uncomfortable.

Search for the Exact Image or Thought

Get specific about what you are envisioning when you say to yourself, "I am dying!" or "I am going crazy!" or "I am losing control!" and then begin a process of asking "What happens next?" until you cannot go any further. This method is not intended to make you feel worse; the key is going through the thought to the other side.

For example, let's look at the catastrophizing statement "I am dying." Find an exact image—the one you play in your mind like a movie—of what you really fear: collapsing in the street, being taken to the emergency room, and so on. (It's not unusual for people to find that, despite their fear of dying, they do not have any specific image of what would happen if they were.) So let's say you imagine yourself collapsing. Now ask yourself, "What happens next?" (Asking this question is very important, so if you find you cannot do it alone, have someone help by asking you the question, repeatedly, in a gentle way.) The next step might be "they hook me up to machines" or "my chest hurts more" or "I am blacking out." Keep on asking "then what happens?" until you get to "then I die." *Then, ask yourself again*: "What happens next?" You would not be alone if you laugh when you realize that the panic would at least be over. But there's a good chance that you will understand more about what the panic means to you or what the fear that leads you to believe you are dying is.

Figure 7.6 shows how this worked for one person who suffered panic. His worries were about losing his job and running out of money because he had no substantial savings, but his panic focused on fears of dying. My remarks to him are in brackets.

By pursuing his thoughts all the way through dying, this man was able to see that what he feared was his financial challenge—the catastrophic thought "I am dying!" was a distraction from (and certainly not a help in) addressing his real problems.

Now let's look at the catastrophizing statement "I am losing control!" If you fear losing control, ask yourself, "If someone were observing me, what exactly would I look like? What would I be doing or saying?" Imagine this in detail. See yourself as if someone else were reporting on your *behavior*, not on your *feelings*. Keep asking the question, every time you describe one action, "Then what?"—all the way through to the end of the panic attack. A typical progression might be something like this: A mother who won't go on a field trip with her daughter

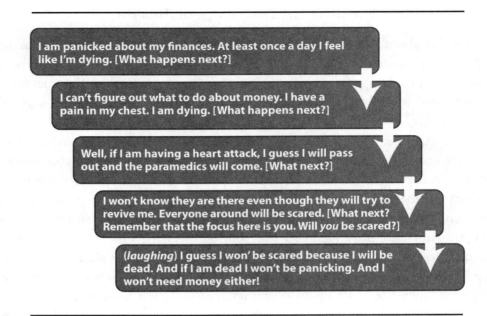

Figure 7.6 One Man's Catastrophe

because she fears panicking on the bus might imagine herself short of breath, looking wild-eyed. When she asks herself "then what?" she might respond with "I would run off the bus!"—as if that is proof of losing control. When asked the question "then what?" again, she might feel confused, wondering, "Isn't that enough?" But, pondering it further, she might find a way to get back on the bus or come to the realization that the other parents can manage the field trip without her.

By using this question again and again to walk yourself through to the end of the attack, you may well recognize that your fear of losing control is invalid.

Finally, let's look at the catastrophizing statement "I am going crazy!" Of all the fears, this one is least likely to have a vivid realistic image. Usually people are only aware that some part of them is afraid that panic means they are crazy. But visualizing a specific image helps here, too. Ask yourself, "What does going crazy look like?" Again, run through the image like a movie, pursuing it until the panic is ended, as I've described. When you know what underlies the fear of being crazy, you will know how to resolve that fear and be less likely to catastrophize.

Following is a blank diagram for you to fill out. In the uppermost box,

The 10 Best-Ever Anxiety Management Techniques Workbook

write in your version of the catastrophic exclamation "I am dying, going crazy, or losing control!" (This process also works well for social anxiety, with the catastrophic exclamation being something like "I will be humiliated!") Then, for each of the subsequent boxes, ask yourself, "What happens next?" and write in your answers. This will help you debunk your fears and stop catastrophizing.

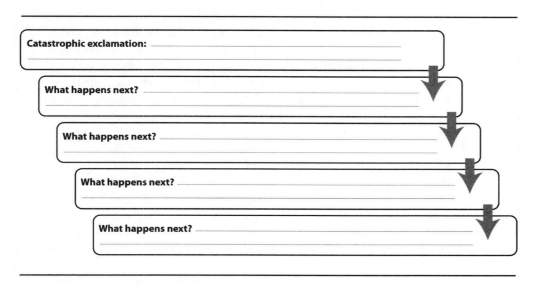

PLAN TO PANIC

It's very easy for people to become afraid of the thing they were doing when they felt panic. For example, if you panic while you are driving on a highway in the rain, you are likely to feel afraid of panicking the next time you are driving in the rain. Subsequently, you might panic not only when you are driving on the highway in the rain, but also any time it rains and any time you are driving no matter how dry the road.

It might seem logical to try to figure out ways to avoid panicking, but this only makes things worse. A better approach is to prepare to panic and plan how to cope with it. It's unlikely that you'll be able to anticipate every potential trigger of panic, so just plan on panicking.

Preparation involves eight simple steps. Check these off as you complete them.

☐ 1. Learn to breathe away panic (Technique #2).
☐ 2. Review each step of the situation that you have been avoiding (Technique #8).
☐ 3. Desensitize every aspect of the situation that you fear could trigger you (Techniques #8 and #10). Note any aspect of the activity that caused you to feel nervous and apply a method to calm down while imagining it. (Systematic desensitization, EMDR, energy therapy, and other methods can help you imagine the aspect of the situation that makes you feel panicky and calm down prior to going into it. See the Recommended Reading and Resources section for more information on therapy methods for desensitizing.)
☐ 4. Practice. Try a mini version of the event or activity. For example, plan to get on one short stretch of highway at a time when there is little traffic and you can get off and go back home or continue on to your destination without using the highway. Stop the practice session at the planned time, even if it is going well.
☐ 5. Write down exactly what you will do if and when you panic. Carry your plan with you in your smartphone or on an index card that you always have with you.
☐ 6. Review your plan before you go into the situation, and have it handy so you can grab it should you panic.
☐ 7. Then try it for real, knowing that if you panic, you have a plan.
☐ 8. Evaluate how it went.
    ☐ Commend yourself for handling difficulties.
    ☐ Praise yourself for doing the whole thing without panic.
    ☐ Decide how to amend your plan if you had a problem.
    ☐ Notice that you lived through it no matter how it went.

LEARN TO KNOW (AND CHOOSE TO SHOW) ANGER

Sometimes anger is so anxiety-producing that people do not even recognize that they feel angry about something. For example:

• You might risk being hurt by someone else if you show you are angry.
• You might not know how to show anger without behaving in a

way that would bother you. For example, if you tend to yell or swear or speak harshly, you may try to avoid being angry in an attempt to avert these behaviors.

- If you have been hurt, abused, or emotionally rejected in the past, feelings of anger may bring back memories of those experiences, which produce anxiety. Thus, you decide that it's better to not feel anger.
- If you were raised to believe anger is wrong, bad, or sinful, you may not want to even know you feel anger.
- If you are angry at someone you love or need (such as a spouse or boss), you may rightly fear you will compromise or lose that relationship if you express your anger.

Does any of this sound familiar to you? If it does, then even *feeling* anger may seem like a catastrophe, and denying that you feel angry—even to yourself—becomes a mechanism to stay safe.

> Hint: Knowing you are angry is not the same as showing you are angry. You can learn safe ways to show anger.

What does this have to do with anxiety? Veronica was convinced that anger had nothing to do with her anxiety. Yet week after week, she told me about things that would have made anyone angry: Her husband forgot she needed the car and he drove to work instead of taking the train, stranding her at home all day. Her daughter brought her 2-year-old twins over for a visit and then asked Veronica to keep them overnight so she could go meet friends. Every time Veronica recounted a situation like these, she explained it away as not being that bad. But as the incidents built up into a pattern, she found herself feeling unappreciated, taken advantage of, and, yes, angry! When it occurred to her that she was angry, her anxiety level immediately dropped.

When you are aware that something is causing anger, you will feel the anger, not the anxiety. You might need time to learn and practice anger management, conflict resolution, negotiating, assertiveness, and other skills that will help you use anger productively in your life, but the first step is recognizing that anger is the feeling you have.

Six Steps for Decatastrophizing Anger

This method is not about showing anger. It is about *knowing* anger. Knowing you are angry is not the same as showing you are angry. The goal is to reduce anxiety by identifying when anxiety masks anger. After becoming aware that anger may be present, you can learn how to handle it.

The method is simple. When you are in the grip of strong sensations of tension, worry, stomach-squeezing doom, and the like—especially when they come on rather suddenly—look for unrecognized anger underneath the anxiety.

Step #1. The next time you feel strong anxiety, immediately sit down and, in single words or brief phrases, write as long a list as possible in answer to this *specific* question: "If I were angry, *what might I be angry about?*" The hypothetical nature of the question is a key feature. You do not have to feel committed to being angry about anything once it's on the list—you are only being speculative about it. Use the following diagram to compile a list of hypothetical things that might anger you. Write ideas in the boxes. These can be things that are big or small, recent or from long ago. You can decide later if it is true that you are angry about any of them.

Step #2. Reflect on what it felt like to write the list. How does it feel to see what you have? What happened to your anxiety level?

Step #3. Review the list. Is there anything on the list that needs action? What can you let go?

Step #4. If something requires action because you are being hurt, taken advantage of, ignored, or worse, talk over your intended action with someone so that you do not put yourself at risk with a badly handled situation. After all, you were feeling your anger as anxiety, so there is a good chance you might not be good at handling anger.

Step #5. Consider skill-building for expressing anger. Learning to be assertive instead of aggressive is a good start for people who are either reluctant or excessive in expressing anger.

Step #6. You can then destroy the list or discuss it in therapy. I ask my clients to discuss with me their reactions to writing this list, and if they feel comfortable it can be helpful to hear the whole list. When they do review the list and their reactions to writing it, they gain insight into the connection between anger and anxiety. This opens the door to deeper levels of psychotherapy to resolve psychological problems with being angry.

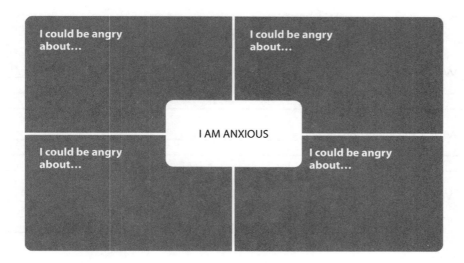

Learn *How* to Be Angry

Once you know you are angry, you may have to figure out *how* to be angry. If you've had bad experiences with being angry in the past, you may not have gained much practice in appropriately expressing anger. You may either blow up or be too quiet, both of which are ineffective. If you know that you are prone to excessive anger (anxiety can prompt some pretty startling displays of excessive anger), seek some guidance from anger-management books to learn to tone down that angry expression. There are also excellent books on assertiveness if you worry that you don't express anger openly enough.

S.I.M.P.L.E. PLAN TO STOP CATASTROPHIZING

Your S.I.M.P.L.E. plan is just a way to decide where to start. Using the tools and methods outlined in this chapter, you can begin to lessen every kind of anxiety you feel. Fill in the following plan with your idea of how to identify your catastrophic thinking and then interrupt it. For example, you might plan to listen to Track 5 on the CD, "Stop Catastrophic Thinking" for several days until you feel sure you will remember the replacement thoughts.

S.I.M.P.L.E. Plan to Stop Catastrophizing

S: What is the *symptom* or *catastrophic thought?* _____
_____
_____

I: What is the *impact* on my life? _____
_____
_____

M: What *method* am I trying? _____
_____
_____

P: *Practice* plan. _____
_____

L: *Lifework.* _____
_____
_____

E: *Evaluate.* _____
_____
_____

A FINAL WORD

Stopping every sort of catastrophizing will take you a long way in managing your anxious mind. These different ways you immediately go to the "oh, no!" or "uh, oh!" in any situation can trigger anxiety—from intense panic to uptight tension. By practicing the methods of this technique, you will be able to sidestep experiences of anxiety before they start or calm them down quickly if they do crop up.

EIGHT

Technique #6: Stop Anxious Thoughts

People experience anxiety because they are set up by biology or life experience to feel anxious even when nothing is objectively wrong. This means that anxiety is a condition looking for content. If you feel anxious, your thoughts start to look around for the reason. Readers with generalized anxiety symptoms know what this feels like, even if they have not previously recognized the searching quality of their anxious thoughts. This process also occurs for people with panic and social anxiety. Any type of anxiety affects thinking. In this chapter you engage in healthy, realistic thinking to override the unhealthy, unrealistic thoughts that plague you.

Consider the state of anxiety. It is a normal emotional reaction in the face of ambiguity. Anxiety is the emotional and physical state that results when you do not know what is happening, what will happen, or what to do about what is happening. That state of anxious arousal demands resolution. If you are experiencing anxiety you want to get rid of it—*pronto*! So what do you do? You move into "what if" thinking mode. You try to figure out what is happening, what will happen, or what you should do about what is happening. If you can figure it out, your anxiety will diminish.

"What if" thinking is a reasonable response to anxiety. Anxious thoughts become an attempt to get rid of anxiety, because if you can figure out what is going on and what to do about it, the ambiguity is resolved. Then you can take action to solve the problem you figured out. For example, suppose you're having a lot of anxiety about starting college. Your "what if" thoughts might be: "What if I can't stand my roommate? What if I can't make friends? What if the workload is too much for me to handle?" These "what if" thoughts can be helpful, because there are ways you can address them: You can call the school to get your roommate's contact information and send an email to the person to begin the introduction process. You can look into extracurricular groups you might be able to join to begin to make friends. You can go through the course catalogue and select a group of courses that will give you a balanced workload.

But what if you feel anxiety for no good reason? What if you feel it simply because of your genetic makeup or because ongoing stress has triggered "free-floating" anxiety (anxiety not connected to real-life events). This is when those "what if" thoughts begin to cause trouble: Because there is no *real* problem, you start creating unreasonable "what if" scenarios. "What if my husband dies in a car accident?" "What if I lose my job and can't support my family?" These thoughts are your brain's effort to get rid of unpleasant anxiety, but if your husband is not, in fact, in imminent danger of dying in a car accident, and if there isn't any real risk of losing your job, then the "what if" thinking does *not* resolve the anxiety—in fact, it makes it worse. Now your thoughts are crowded with *potential* problems that only *might* be issues. And your anxiety gets worse because the "what if" thinking has created real ambiguity. You feel bad, you do not know why, and you cannot figure it out. This is how "what if" thinking increases in a vicious circle.

An anxiety disorder is not an outcome of your thinking, but rather the other way around. Excessive anxious thinking is an outcome of an anxiety disorder. And here is the dilemma. When your anxiety is not a reaction to a real-life scenario, then the ensuing "what if" thinking worsens the anxiety. The same process occurs with panic and social anxiety, as those conditions are also initiated by conditions in your brain. For example, if you have a panic attack or experience embarrassment in a social setting, you associate the activity you were doing with the panic or social embarrassment, and then when that activity comes up, you begin to think, "What if I panic or mess up?" You begin to think about the consequences, and those thoughts lead to more anxiety.

Of course, when you have "what if" thoughts that aren't connected to any real-life situation, you eventually realize they were wrong. Your husband got home (again) without having a car accident. You were able to go grocery shopping without panicking. You got through the birthday party without making any major social blunders. Realizing this, you feel somewhat better. But then, because your brain is primed to feel anxiety without a real-life cause, you start to feel the anxious thoughts all over again and begin another cycle of "what if" thinking. Again, this kind of anxiety is a condition looking for content.

When you can begin to see this pattern in yourself, you are on the path to recovery. Once you have noticed that your anxious thoughts did not come to pass and the anxiety was unnecessary, you can say to yourself, every time a new worry pops up, "Aha! A new anxiety! I don't have to believe this is any truer than any of my previous 'what if' thoughts!"

ASSESS YOURSELF

Anxious thoughts can be very convincing, even when they aren't connected to any real-life problem.

Are You Plagued by Anxious, "What If" Thoughts?

Check off all of the following statements that describe you.

☐ I am constantly wondering if I have bothered people at home or work.

☐ I often wonder if physical sensations I have could be signs of a disease.

☐ I spend time researching symptoms on the Internet to reassure myself that I am not sick.

☐ I review my work and my calendar repeatedly to see whether I have forgotten or missed something important.

☐ I spend hours or days feeling anxious, as if something bad is about to happen. (I wait for the "other shoe" to drop.)

☐ When someone calls me or says in person that he or she wants to talk, I immediately assume I will be chastised, fired, or told I have done something wrong.

☐ I have often gotten rid of one anxious thought only to have another pop up with the same intensity.

If you make a mistake, no matter how small, do any of these apply to you?

☐ I think over and over about what bad things can happen when I make a mistake.

☐ If I make a mistake at work, I spend hours worrying if I will get into serious trouble, even if I am not sure anyone has noticed it.

☐ If I suspect I have made a social error, such as forgetting a name, dropping food on someone's carpet, or laughing when someone was being serious, I think that friends will talk about me or stop liking me. I can feel sick for days about it.

☐ I have anxious thoughts for days or even weeks prior to an activity during which I might have a panic or social-anxiety attack.

☐ I think about mistakes I made in the past and wonder if I could still get into trouble now.

If you checked any of the boxes in these two lists, do the following thought-stopping method when you notice anxious thoughts coming on. If you checked 3 or more boxes, it means that anxious thoughts are interfering with your life and you might need all the various interventions that go with thought-stopping.

There are many methods you can employ to conquer anxious thinking. As you review the methods below, consider which fit your thought pattern best and start with those. As you begin to control anxious thoughts, you will eventually recognize how fear and anxiety trigger thoughts and how you can intervene on the sensations of anxiety and fear before you are caught up in yet another "what if" thinking scenario.

THOUGHT-STOPPING AND THOUGHT REPLACEMENT

The basic model for ridding yourself of anxious thoughts is the thought-stopping and thought replacement method, which has many permutations and applications.

The first step is to recognize the tricks that anxiety plays on your mind. As mentioned earlier, anxious thoughts can be very convincing, but you need to learn to tell yourself: *My anxious thoughts are not true or valid.* (Again, this is for times when the anxious thoughts are not connected to a real-life problem. If your house actually *is* burning down, or your boss actually *did* put you on probation, then your anxious thoughts are perfectly reasonable. The key is recognizing the difference between something that is *actually happening now* and what anxiety is *tricking* you into believing *might* be happening or *could* happen.)

If you cannot do that, you must spend time understanding why you think your anxious thought is useful and *challenge that assumption* until you are clear that the thought is worthless to you. For example, suppose you are worried that your husband is planning on leaving you—despite a lack of evidence proving he's dissatisfied with the relationship—and no matter how hard you try, you can't shake these thoughts. Ask yourself, "Why do I think this anxious thought is useful?" Perhaps it's because it makes you feel like you'll be more prepared for the bad news if or when it comes. Now challenge that assumption. Will you be any less able to pack your belongings and find a new place to live if you *haven't* been worrying that he's going to leave you? Will you be any less devastated about the breakup? No! In fact, your constant worrying might even be taking a toll on him and making the situation worse. Your anxious thoughts are worthless to you.

The second step is to tell yourself firmly to "stop!" whenever you notice anxious thinking. You must interrupt the negativity as quickly as you can, and do it every time you notice a negative thought pop up.

Figure 8.1 Thought-Stopping and Thought Replacement

The last step is to immediately change the direction of your thoughts. I'll discuss this step of thought replacement more thoroughly a bit later.

Figure 8.1 shows the process in a nutshell.

Why must you interrupt your negativity every single time you think the worry thought? In The *10 Best-Ever Anxiety Management Techniques* and *The Anxious Brain* I describe this process more fully, but basically, every time you think a thought, it is easier for your brain to think that thought again. You develop strong pathways in your brain that need to be erased. Every time you stop the thought without continuing it, you weaken the trace until it is eventually erased. Erasing the trace means you will be less likely to have that anxious thought in the future.

Hint: Be persistent! *Your worry might fight back and actually increase for a day or two before lessening dramatically.*

But—and this is a *big* but—the thought will bounce right back if you have nothing to replace it with. So you must plan ahead for good thought replacements. Following are some good ways of doing thought replacement.

- Singing (Yes! It is a great choice because your whole brain gets busy when you sing.)
- Picking a pleasant or productive thought to focus on for the day, such as remembering a fun, recent outing to the park with your grandchildren, or deciding what restaurant you'd like to eat out at this weekend.
- Listening to music or an audio book
- Reciting an inspirational verse or mantra

- Returning your attention carefully back to the work you are doing when the anxious thought strikes

Why is planning thought replacement so necessary? An especially ruminative anxious thinker, Christy, remarked, "This thought-replacement thing does not make sense to me. Why does it work? Every time I stop one negative thought, another negative thought pops up to take its place!" She had missed the part where she had to plan for a *positive* thought replacement! Figure 8.2 is an example of how this works.

MOVE YOUR BODY, MOVE YOUR MIND

A very important aspect of thought-stopping and thought replacing is helping the stuck brain move into more productive thinking. Moving your body can help enormously with this, especially if you have panic or social anxiety. "Move a muscle, move a thought" is another way to phrase this. The stuck brain literally starts to move when your muscles move, and if you couple the movement with a thought-replacement technique, so much the better. Here are some ideas for moving your body:

- Listen to Track 6 on the CD to "Shake It Off."
- Do something around the house, especially if you have been sitting at the computer or television—put in a load of laundry, wash a dish, walk the dog, tidy up a room.

Figure 8.2 Planning Thought Replacement

- At work, take a walk down the hall, go to the water fountain, or walk up and down steps in a stairwell for a minute while thinking about the work task you will do when you get back to your work station.
- For children, make a "kid grid" (like a tic-tac-toe chart) of nine things they can do without their parents for 15 minutes or so. Then, when they are anxious, parents can direct them to their list of things to do instead.

FIND YOUR TYPE OF "WHAT IF" THINKING

Thought-stopping and thought replacement work well with all kinds of anxious thoughts. But different types of "what if" thinking present different kinds of challenges and therefore require different adaptations of the thought-stopping and thought replacement method. The following sections describe different kinds of anxious thinking and offer ways of adapting this method to each.

Rumination and "What If" Thinking With a Theme

Hint: Notice if any of your "what if" thinking helped you or if any of those thoughts came true!

"Ruminate" means to think something over and over. I grew up in dairy country and we all knew about ruminative animals such as cows. Their digestive process is to ingest, digest, and then redigest food by bringing it up to chew on for a while, then swallowing it again, then bringing it up to chew on again. Anxious thoughts can be like that. You think the same thought over and over, even though nothing about the thought changes when you do. You chew on an idea without resolving it or solving it.

Remember, anxiety is a condition looking for content. Yesterday your thoughts might have been stuck on whether something you said was misinterpreted. Today you might be stuck on whether you planned your budget the right way. Tomorrow you might fret all day about whether you took your pill and wonder if you should take one now, risking a double dose—never making an actual decision but rather fretting the day away. Ruminations can change rapidly, but the distinctive feature is that your mind is always going over and over a thought without finishing it.

Sometimes ruminative thinkers get stuck on specific topics, such as whether they have offended others, have made mistakes at work, have a disease, have hurt a pet or child in some way (often by failure to attend to a need rather than by hurting the pet or child physically and deliberately), or have failed to notice some important detail. Omission of a necessary action can be seen as being as bad as committing a wrong. People who ruminate with a theme tend to be okay when not reminded of their problem, but they also believe that if they could just resolve this one situation, they won't be anxious again. Sadly, that is rarely true. They may get a brief spell of relief, but then, because anxiety is a condition looking for content, some other "what if" thought will arrive to explain the sensation of anxiety.

Do You Suffer from Rumination with a Theme?
Make a list of all the things you've fretted about in the last month.

1. _____
2. _____
3. _____
4. _____
5. _____
6. _____

Help for Rumination and "What If" Thinking With a Theme

If your ruminations have a theme, there is an additional and vital step to insert in the thought-stopping and thought replacement method. For some people, the theme of their ruminative thinking relates to an actual life experience. For example, if you had a parent with a chronic illness, you might be hyper-alert to signs of that illness in yourself. This can make letting go of the anxious thought especially difficult. You might feel you are being disloyal to your parent, or you might believe that not worrying is tempting fate to give you the illness.

When this is the case, these kinds of thoughts must be identified and resolved before thought-stopping can work.

The following diagram provides space for you to identify a rumination and plan a thought replacement to try. Remember to try it for a minimum of a week to see the change. Initially, your "what if" thinking may increase a bit to challenge your resolve, but it will then drop off precipitously if you are very persistent in erasing the trace and replacing it.

The ruminative thought:

_____
_____
_____
_____

• Decide the thought is not valuable and say "stop!"

REPLACEMENTS:

•_____
•_____
•_____

Home-or-Workplace-in-Danger Thoughts

This is basically the "did I leave something turned on?" scenario, which is a type of "what if" thinking. There are many variations in addition to the "did I turn off the coffee pot/stove/lights/curling iron" version: "Did I lock the doors?" "Did I close the windows?" "Did I blow out the candle?" "Did I bring in the dog?" This type of thinking is often the result of inattentiveness due to the preoccupied or frantic thought process typical of a revved-up, anxious mind. These types of worriers do not stay in the here-and-now but rather rush ahead with thoughts like "What if traffic is bad this morning?" or "How will I get all my work done today?" or "How did I not notice how late it is?" Distracted by these thoughts, these worriers fail to pay attention to what they are doing in the present. As they leave work or home, preoccupied with worry, they do the leaving-for-the-day tasks on automatic pilot, and once they're on the road, the "what if" thinking strikes. It is accompanied by a sinking feeling in the stomach or an instantaneous flare of tingling fear. And now they are beset by two scenarios of trouble: "What if I don't go back and check?" and "What if I lose the time to go back and check?" It is a no-win situation, and they can remain preoccupied by see-sawing between two bad choices.

Have you gone back to check or thought repetitively about leaving things on at home or work? Fill out the following diagram to identify your places and types of "what if" thinking.

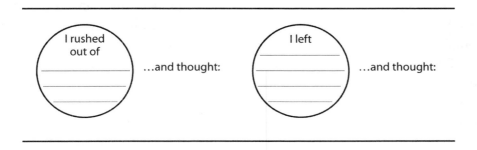

Help for Home-or-Workplace-in-Danger Thoughts

There is only one really good fix for this kind of anxiety because it is caused by inattention from being preoccupied. You must pay attention—*especially when you are already rushed and anxious.* So this is truly a simple method. Whenever you make a transition from home or from your workplace, especially when you are rushed, pay attention out loud. See Figure 8.3.

Steps to Pay Attention Out Loud

1. As you get ready to leave, take a breath and start noticing what you are doing.
2. Say to yourself out loud, "Look at this—the cord to the iron is in my hand," or "I am holding the keys I will lock the door with," or "I've got every file off of my desk that I need to take home."
3. If you are forgetful about routines you need to follow when leaving home or your workplace, make a list. It can be a one-time list, such as everything you need to do to get ready for a vacation, or a more routine list that includes everything you need to do before leaving for work or leaving for home.
4. As you are about to leave, pause. Take a deep breath. Ask yourself, "Is there anything else?"
5. Now pay attention to where you are going!

Figure 8.3 Steps to Pay Attention Out Loud

Hypochondria-Like Thoughts

This is about having some kind of physical symptom and becoming afraid that it is a sign of a deadly disease. Every headache turns into a brain tumor, every sore throat is cancer, every little skin rash becomes a flesh-eating bacteria. If you are beset by this kind of "what if" thinking, you are wishing I would stop listing examples here—you don't need any new concerns to think about!

This kind of "what if" thinking gets even more problematic when you begin researching your symptoms on the Internet. You either waste a lot of time or really scare yourself when you find all of the possibilities for what your symptoms could mean. It also gets to be a problem if you run to the doctor with every new symptom "just to be sure." You may get relief from anxiety that way, but it will be costly in time and money.

Watching television can further exacerbate the problem. Commercial breaks are full of advertisements for drugs that treat countless conditions you've never even heard of, and infomercials drone on about how you should better your health by taking a supplement or vitamin or by trying a new regimen of exercise with the equipment they're selling. Many news programs feature stories about diseases you might catch, your risk of exposure to contaminants, or whatever the healthy "superfood" of the moment is. Next week they will report on how all of this was wrong or harmful. Anyone who takes everything we heard in the media seriously could end up overly focused on health and any little sniffle or pain might seem dangerous.

Help for Hypochondria-Like Thoughts

The key is knowing when to take your symptoms seriously and when to recognize that your fears are exaggerated. Once you've recognized that your fears are exaggerated, you must use thought-stopping and thought replacement to eliminate them. See Figure 8.4. You may need a helper to listen to you go through these a time or two.

Too-Much-To-Do Rumination

There are times in life when the need to accomplish tasks is truly burdensome. You might be working and also going to school, or you might be a single parent needing to work for income as well as raise children. However, people who

Steps to Eliminate Hypochondria-Like Thoughts

1. Get it out in the open. Sometimes hearing your fear aloud makes it seem ridiculous.
2. Do not go on the Internet to research. If a condition is serious at this moment, you will have indisputable indicators: significant pain or signs like high fever, out-of-control vomiting, bleeding, fainting, and so on. These are physical signs that cannot be ignored—indications that you should seek help right now. You don't need to research them.
3. For lesser symptoms that trouble you because they *might* be something, ask yourself, "What would be the signs that this symptom is important?" Write them down until you get the hang of this step. This would include simple awareness that the condition is worsening. For example, a rash might spread or become painful or a fever might persist. You might need to ask someone for input while you get better at this.
4. Decide when you will evaluate your symptoms again. For example, you might decide to check on your rash in 3 hours and if it is still the same, you'll check it again 24 hours later. Do not keep checking beyond that agreement with yourself on when to check.
5. Do not seek reassurance from others—rather, seek information. For example: "I am worried about whether I should take medicine for my allergies. I heard it can be hard on my heart and I don't know if that is true." Identify one knowledgeable person you could ask about that.
6. Then do the thought-stopping and thought replacement as described earlier.

Figure 8.4 Steps to Eliminate Hypochondria-Like Thoughts

have difficulty prioritizing work, planning, or following through (as you might if you have attention-deficit disorder) may feel overwhelmed even without an exceptional burden of extra work. Either scenario can lead to anxiety and panic.

One of my clients, Brock, felt that he had fallen apart since starting an internship at school. He was expected to quickly learn all the tasks the job entailed and deal with all the new people at the job site. At the same time, he had a pile of journals to read for his internship seminar class. He felt panicky and was plagued by "what if I fail?" thinking. To deal with his stress, he began playing video games—often for hours at a time—which did provide a distraction and give him some relief, but obviously didn't solve his problem of having too much to do. Brock needed a plan to get his work done, he needed to prioritize his tasks, and he needed to get started. Only then would his anxiety diminish.

Make a Plan

The best solution to this kind of unproductive thinking is learning how to plan and prioritize. The following chapter goes into detail about planning. I only mention it here in the context of "what if" thinking because it is common for people who ruminate to review a situation over and over without deciding how they will handle it. A good plan will eliminate unnecessary thinking, but there is one caveat: Once you make a plan, follow it to its end point! Do not revise your plan over and over—that is just "what if" anxious thinking in disguise.

Do the Worst First

This one little method can help a lot to stop your fretting. The slogan "do the worst first" is a simple reminder to do what you do *not* want to do, but which you must do, as soon as possible. If you are going to worry all day about what you have to do (like make a phone call you don't want to make, or pay the bills), just do it first and save the worry. What a relief! There are four simple steps to follow.

1. Identify what you are putting off and notice how much you think about it.
2. Then decide when exactly you are going to do what you have been putting off.
3. Now do it!
4. Finally, notice how you feel when it is off your mind.

Fill out the following diagram to help you do the worst first.

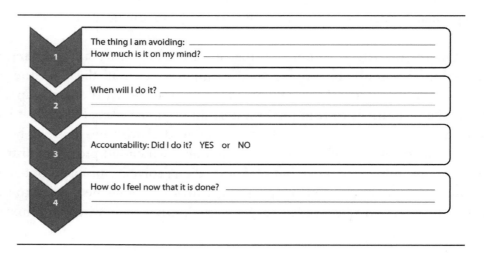

The 10 Best-Ever Anxiety Management Techniques Workbook

List With Time Frames

1. List everything you have to get done. If a task requires several days to complete (such as grading your English students' final exams) break it down into smaller units (such as reading and grading just five exams).
2. Next to each item, list how long it will take (in minutes). If it involves traveling someplace, like picking up dry cleaning, include the transportation time.
3. Then prioritize the list, numbering each task, with #1 being the highest priority.
4. Now, identify how much time you have in the day to devote to the items on your list (in minutes).
5. Finally, draw a line under the items that will use up the amount of available time you have.
6. Once you know your limit, you can relax your expectation to do more. That is all you can do for one day.

Figure 8.5 List With Time Frames

Make a List With Time Frames

Parents, people who work two jobs, people who work and go to school—all face a multitude of tasks that will at some point seem like too much to do. If this applies to you, consider creating a list with time frames to keep your expectations of yourself reasonable and your anxiety at bay. False expectations about how much you can do will usually make you anxious, and this kind of list is the best remedy.

Begin by making an accurate appraisal of how long (in minutes) each thing will take, and then prioritize what items are most important. When you can identify how much is possible for you to get done in a day, you can have accurate expectations about your day. Prioritizing your tasks resolves the frantic feelings about what you are not getting done. The basic steps are listed in Figure 8.5.

You may be skeptical, but there is power in this kind of list: It makes you face reality. If you cannot get a task done, then you cannot get it done. If you have a list far longer than can be accomplished in a single day, try the following adjustments:

1. Remove items with later deadlines. Keep a separate list for those.
2. If, when you see what you are *not* going to do on the day's list, you react by saying, "Oh, no! I *have* to get that done by today!" (for instance, return a pile of library books due that day), then you need

to change your priorities to accommodate what is most pressing. It is also possible that you will have to deal with the reality that you may miss a deadline. That may involve asking others for an adjustment or extension or telling someone you won't be able to complete an expected task. It can be a great relief to admit you are not going to get something done and set a new, more reasonable deadline.

3. Do not focus on what you cannot do. Just focus on what you will get done and feel good about it.

S.I.M.P.L.E. PLAN TO STOP ANXIOUS THOUGHTS

You will do yourself a favor if you start working to eliminate "what if" thinking right away. Pick one type of anxious thinking to start with, and make a S.I.M.P.L.E. plan that incorporates one of the methods listed in this chapter. Figure 8.6 shows a sample S.I.M.P.L.E. plan; a blank one for you to fill out follows it.

S.I.M.P.L.E. Plan to Stop Anxious Thoughts

S: What is the *symptom or situation*? _My "what if" concerns are totally preoccupying my thoughts about the new car I got. What if I paid too much? What if it has a recall? What if I find there was a much better choice for me? You name it, I am thinking about it!_

I: What is the *impact* on my life? _I get another thought like this every time I get into the car, and every time people mention cars, I get a sick feeling. I can't even enjoy the new car._

M: What *method* am I trying? _I am going to do thought-stopping and thought replacement, and I am going to write a Post-It note every morning to remind myself to think about something pleasant whenever I notice I am thinking about the car._

Figure 8.6 S.I.M.P.L.E. Plan to Stop Anxious Thoughts

P: Practice plan. *I will spend a minute every morning writing at least two positive things to think about. Then I will say them out loud once to myself. I will remind myself once each morning that my "what if" thinking is a waste of time.*

L: Lifework. *I will post the note on my cash register at work and on the dashboard of my car so that I see it and can remind myself of my goal.*

E: Evaluate. *After each week I will see if I am able to ride in my car or hear people mention cars without feeling bad.*

Figure 8.6 Continued

S.I.M.P.L.E. Plan to Stop Anxious Thoughts

S: What is the *symptom* or *situation?* _____
_____
_____

I: What is the *impact* on my life? _____
_____
_____

M: What *method* am I trying? _____
_____
_____

P: *Practice* plan. _____
_____
_____

L: Lifework. _____
_____
_____

E: Evaluate. _____
_____
_____

A FINAL WORD

Everyone has experienced "what if" thinking at some point. Life sometimes throws us situations that are genuinely troubling or that are likely to result in serious trouble. But there are times when our "what if" thinking gets out of hand—when it has little or nothing at all to do with reality. "What if I break my back and get paralyzed on the football field tonight?" "What if my 3-year-old grows up to be a drug addict?" In reality, most "what if" thinking is a waste of time and only reinforces anxiety.

Regardless of whether the "what if" thinking is about something real or is just the result of your anxious brain, the question is *how much* your anxious thoughts take up your mental time and make you feel worse. Remember that "what if" thinking is an effort to resolve anxiety (albeit an effort that doesn't work, as a new anxious thought will pop up after you've resolved the previous one). The challenge is to stop the anxious thought and replace it with a productive one that *will* eliminate anxiety. Using the methods in this technique should provide you with relief and bring you back into a life free of anxiety.

The 10 Best-Ever Anxiety Management Techniques Workbook

NINE

Technique #7: Contain Your Worry

Everybody worries, but people with generalized anxiety elevate worry to an art form. They take normal worries and develop them into monstrous impediments to clear thinking, enlarging them out of proportion to reality by excessive rumination. As you worry, you might even fear you are crazy because the kinds of things you're concerned about become so excessive. Your logical brain knows the things you worry about are unlikely to happen, but in your gut you feel as if they could. Containing the worry to one time or one topic may seem an impossible hurdle, but there are effective ways to do just that, with relief from anxiety being the welcome result.

The intensity of these kinds of worries is due to the highly active brain commonly seen in people with generalized anxiety. That active brain actively worries. But your active brain can help you, too—giving you the energy to remain persistent in *controlling* your worry.

Worry is insistent. It feels important. But when you persistently work against it, worry abates. That is the goal of this chapter: to get worry back down to normal proportions.

ASSESS YOURSELF

Out-of-control worry isn't just a nuisance—it can negatively affect your entire life, interfering with everyday functioning and robbing you of the pleasure you once felt in doing things you enjoy.

Do You Need to Contain Your Worry?

Check off all the statements that describe you.

☐ My worry is hard to control; it creeps into my thoughts all day.
☐ I am so preoccupied with my worries that I rarely feel joy anymore.
☐ I cannot pay attention. My worry interferes with attention for the details that enrich or inform life.

Total number of boxes checked _____

☐ I spend a lot of time feeling concerned about the outcome of projects I undertake at home or work.
☐ I worry that every fever and cough my child has is going to escalate into a life-threatening illness.
☐ Whenever I hear about a potential health risk from a food (such as artery-clogging saturated fats), I immediately stop eating it and get it out of the house.
☐ I have worried about whether I've fed guests food that might cause food poisoning.
☐ I have worried that I will be put in jail for mistakes on income-tax forms or failure to comply with some detail that has legal repercussions.
☐ I've had serious concerns about becoming homeless, even though I am well educated and have a good job that I'm not currently in danger of losing.
☐ I cope quite well with real, even disastrous, problems.

Total number of boxes checked _____

If you checked one of the boxes in the first list, you will want to use the methods presented in this chapter. If you checked two or more boxes in the second list, pay *special* attention to all the methods in this chapter and seriously consider getting additional support in your effort to be persistent about containing your worry.

When a person is no longer able to shrug off worry, it is time to take charge and learn how to manage it. No one can avoid worry altogether in the course of life, but anyone can contain worry. This chapter takes into account the reality that, at times, people cannot just "stop worrying about it," as their family and friends tell them to do. They instead have to employ specific methods to contain their worries.

GET THE RIGHT REASSURANCE

Do you try to calm down by getting reassurance from someone else? Do you ask people to tell you that what you worry about cannot happen? You may believe you won't worry anymore if you can just get the *right* solution or the *right* information, and this leads you to ask other people for reassurance. Essentially you are asking, "Can you tell me my worries are unfounded?" You want to be reassured once and for all, but the reassurance ends up being only temporary. You may feel better for a while, but inevitably another worry crops up.

Typically, people who worry find a flaw in the reassurance: There will always be one factor you forgot to include in the discussion, and now—darn it!— the reassurance is not complete. This is why Internet searching becomes such a time-consuming pastime for worriers. You can search and search without actually bothering your family and friends for reassurance. But reassurance-seeking on the Internet is a trap that makes worry worse and does not teach you how *not* to worry in the future.

The *right* reassurance is reassurance that you are competent to handle problems. You don't feel better when people just tell you everything will be fine without addressing the content of your worry. But you *will* get some relief from your worry if you remind yourself that even if the worst *does* happen, you will be able to deal with it.

At this point, you will need to include others in your effort to contain worry. People you turn to for support and reassurance will need some information to help you make good progress. Getting the right reassurance requires you to give instructions to friends or family. Have them read this portion of the workbook and give them your own, personalized "wrong reassurance versus right reassurance" reminder (the blank form for this follows Figure 9.3).

The following sections describe the right reassurance and wrong reassurance for each type of anxiety.

Reassurance for Generalized Anxiety

For people with generalized anxiety, the first step in securing the right reassurance is getting the worry out in the open to see if it is connected to a real problem or is simply the result of your anxiety looking for content.

Once the problem is defined, the right reassurance consists of ascertaining that you are competent to handle the consequences of your problem: "If it turns out there is a problem, you will figure out what to do." Figure 9.1 gives examples of the right reassurance versus the wrong reassurance.

Reassurance for Panic

The right reassurance for panic is *not*, "Oh, you won't panic." It is: "Even if you do panic, once it is over, you can go on with what you were doing." Or: "Even if you panic, you will get through it." Or: "If you should panic, even if it is a lot of panic, you have all the skills you need to cope with it." Of course, people *do* need the skills to stop panic, so if this reassurance is to be successful, make sure you worked on Chapters 4 (Breathe) and 7 (Stop Catastrophizing).

The first step for getting the right reassurance for panic is to acknowledge that the fear is that: (1) the panic will be *horrible*, and (2) the outcome—dying, going crazy, or losing control—will be *awful*. In fact, neither catastrophe is true.

It may be true that if you panic, you will feel embarrassed or will want to escape, so remind yourself that you have the skills to cope with it.

Finally, remind yourself that you are competent to handle your panic and the consequences of panic. Figure 9.2 gives examples of the right reassurance versus the wrong reassurance for panic.

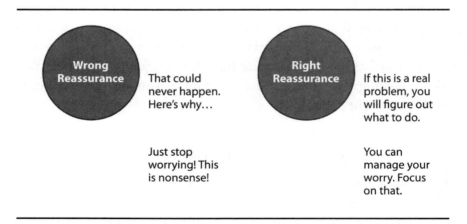

Figure 9.1 Right Reassurance Versus Wrong Reassurance for Generalized Anxiety

The 10 Best-Ever Anxiety Management Techniques Workbook

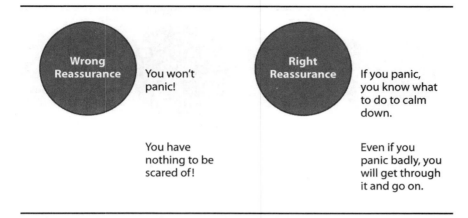

Figure 9.2 Right Reassurance Versus Wrong Reassurance for Panic

Reassurance for Social Anxiety

Because people with social anxiety are especially sensitive to feelings of anxiety, they are more inclined to fear feeling anxious. They particularly fear other people noticing they are nervous. If you have social anxiety symptoms, you will need the social skills to accomplish your goals as well as the practice to make them work well. Pay special attention to Chapters 10–12 to develop and practice a plan.

At the beginning, the right reassurance for people with social anxiety is: "You are working on your goals, and I can help you with that." Once you have worked on your plan and practiced it, your right reassurance might be: "Even if you show some anxiety, you know how to get through it. And remember, people are more accepting than you may think."

In general, the right reassurance for social anxiety includes: (1) Openly acknowledging what *exactly* you think will happen, and (2) reminding yourself that you have the competence to handle both your fear and the consequences of feeling afraid ("You can tolerate feeling afraid, and you can handle it if you look nervous"). Figure 9.3 gives examples of the right reassurance versus the wrong reassurance for social anxiety.

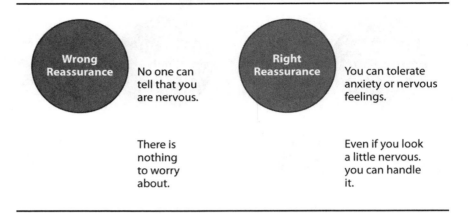

Wrong Reassurance

No one can tell that you are nervous.

There is nothing to worry about.

Right Reassurance

You can tolerate anxiety or nervous feelings.

Even if you look a little nervous. you can handle it.

Figure 9.3 Right Reassurance Versus Wrong Reassurance for Social Anxiety

Write in your own reassurance phrases on the following diagram.

Wrong Reassurance Don't tell me:

_____
_____
_____
_____

Right Reassurance Do tell me:

_____
_____
_____
_____

MAKE A PLAN

People with anxiety are often extremely competent in handling real problems. Real problems have real solutions; with an unambiguous problem and an unambiguous solution, anxiety disappears. (Remember, anxiety is a response to ambiguity.) A clear plan of action is a godsend to an anxious mind. That's why planning is a terrific anti-worry measure.

Consider your typical type of worry: "What if my car breaks down on vacation?" "What if I fail the test?" "What if no one asks me to the prom?" "What if I don't get this job I applied for?" All of these situations have a common element—if they *do* happen, a response will be in order, and in each case, a plan could be made. But worriers sometimes get confused between what might require action and what is just a worry. If you cannot identify a specific problem that can be solved, then you're probably just having an anxious thought, and thought-stopping and thought replacement (see Technique #6) are in order. For example, ruminatively thinking "What if I lose my job?" may be a pointless (though disturbing) worry if you have a secure job in a stable company. But if you are worrying about a *real* situation—"My company is going to lay off 30% of the workforce when this location closes, and one of those people could be me"—then you have an actual possible problem that can be addressed by coming up with a plan.

Even when there *is* a real situation that can be addressed by a plan, however, some people simply worry about the situation without moving to the next step of identifying the actual problem. Mandy was a good example of that. She called in distress, saying, "I lost my job!" and asked for an emergency appointment. When she came in, I asked her what she wanted to discuss. She was taken aback. "I lost my job!" she exclaimed, wondering if I heard her the first time. "Yes," I replied, "but how is that a problem?" With a look of puzzlement on her face, she said carefully, "*I . . . lost . . . my . . . job.*" "Indeed. And how does losing your job cause a problem in your life?" Then it dawned on her: "Oh. Because I lost my job, now I have the problem of needing another source of income." As a reader, you may be thinking, "Well, that's obvious! Losing your job is the same as the problem of needing a new source of income." But don't be quick to leap to such conclusions. Instead, consider Stephanie, who also lost her job. Stephanie had worked at a nonprofit organization that supported the arts. Married to a successful lawyer, she didn't need to work for financial reasons—she worked because it provided her with a sense of purpose in life and because the job gave her status in the community. Both Mandy and Stephanie had lost their jobs, but their *problems* were very different, as were the solutions. To solve *her* problem, Mandy needed to find a new source of income. Stephanie, on the other hand, needed to find a new way to give her life purpose, possibly by doing volunteer work or taking up a new activity. By getting stuck on the *situation*—"I lost my job"—you can feel desperately worried but unable to resolve your anxiety because you haven't defined the problem.

Once you've identified the problem, you can begin figuring out a plan to address it, which will be a big relief to your anxious mind. The final step of the process is evaluating your progress. The following sections describe the whole process in detail.

Identify the Problem

What is the problem? Get very specific—for example: "I want a shot at a scholarship and I have three B's. I want to raise them to A's." Or: "I want to go to the winter dance with a date and I have not yet been asked." Write your problem in the following diagram.

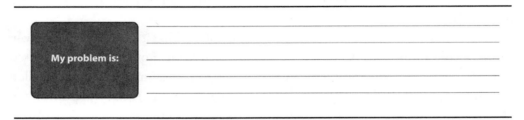

My problem is:

Now, what is the goal? Goals direct solutions. For example, suppose your problem is that you haven't been asked to the winter dance. There could be several different goals associated with this problem. One might be: "I want to go to the dance with John Doe." A very different goal might be: "I don't want to sit at home feeling lonely while my friends are at the dance." Each of these goals would lead to different solutions. In the first case, you might not want to accept any invitation to the dance unless it's from John Doe. In the second, you probably *would* accept any invitation to the dance—or just decide to go without a date. Write your goal in the following diagram.

My goal is:

Brainstorm About Options for Solutions

What are possible solutions to achieve your goal? List every option. Anxiety narrows your thinking because it puts blinders on your attention and creativity. Sometimes listing wrong choices makes it easier to see the right one. A lot of anxiety is generated by feeling you have no choice or control in a situation. But you always have a choice, even if the choice is to continue on the path you are already on.

Another trick your mind might play on you is: "What if I did not think of *everything*?" To circumvent this, ask yourself, before you wrap up action steps, "Is there anything else I have to consider or do?" If you answer, "No, this should cover it all," then your worry "What if I did not think of everything?" is just a trick your anxious brain is playing on you. Say to yourself: "I will not re-plan my plan. I will evaluate my progress on _____." Then do thought replacement.

Write down all the possible solutions to your problem in the following diagram.

Option #1: _____

Option #2: _____

Option #3: _____

Option #4: _____

Option #5: _____
_____
_____
_____

Select One Option

Now pick one "best" solution and identify the action steps you'll need to follow to do it. Remember: You are picking the best solution—not the perfect solution!

People often get stuck worrying, "What if I choose wrong?" But the truth is this: There are many good solutions; there is no perfect solution. Say to yourself instead: "I can change my mind later if my evaluation shows this solution is ineffective." This is the purpose of evaluation!

> Hint: There are many good solutions. There are no perfect solutions. Pick one and go for it!

Write down your solution and the action steps it requires in the following diagram.

Solution: _____

Action step #1: _____

Action step #2: _____

Action step #3: _____

Action step #4: _____

Action step #5: _____

Tell Yourself, "Stop! I Have a Plan!"

Expert worriers may find themselves worrying even *after* they have a plan. This is where thought-stopping comes in. If you feel those "what if" thoughts popping back up, tell yourself "stop!" and then add, "I have a plan!" Then use your planned-ahead thought replacement.

Evaluate How the Plan Is Working

It is necessary to plan evaluation points. If you don't, you will just continue worry: "Is this the right step? Is this working? What if it doesn't work?" Remember, you are evaluating your *progress*—not whether the problem has been completely resolved. Depending on your goal, achieving the solution may take some time. But working *toward* that goal is something you can begin immediately, noting whether you've been successful in achieving each of the action steps on the path to solving the problem. Decide which action steps need evaluation and when.

Here's how to do it:

1. Decide what the first reasonable point to evaluate your progress is, and mark it down on your calendar. For example, if your goal is to find a new job, a reasonable first evaluation point might be in 2 weeks. ("Have I sent out my c.v. to at least five different companies? Have I received any requests for interviews?") If your goal is to mend a friendship with someone you had a falling out with, your first evaluation point might be quite a bit later. *Don't monitor daily unless it is called for*—that's just another way of letting "what if" thinking creep in. If you notice yourself doing this, say, "Stop! I will think about this on _____" and then do thought replacement.

2. If obstacles come up, you can revise your action steps.

3. Evaluate the results on the day you marked down in your calendar.
   a. If you were successful, note what you did to make it work.
   b. If you were unsuccessful, either revise your action steps or consider trying a different solution option.

4. After evaluating your results, set a new evaluation date and mark it on your calendar. Continue with this process until the problem is solved.

My problem:

Solution I will try:

1st
solution

2nd
solution

action
step #1

action
step #2

Evaluate

amend a step

continue to next
step

Figure 9.4 The Process of Making a Good Plan

An Additional Note About Evaluating

In Chapter 10, on changing self-talk, I will discuss how anxiety causes you to look for what is wrong more than what is right. When evaluating your progress toward your goal, look at what is working! What is going right? How did you make that happen? What do you want to adjust to make it better? Stay far away from what is wrong or not perfect.

Figure 9.4 shows a short form of the entire planning process.

WORRY WELL AND ONLY ONCE

People with anxiety disorders worry when worry is unnecessary, worry when there is no value in worrying, and, mostly, worry to the extent that it ruins their lives. "Worry Well and Only Once" is a method that takes worry seriously *one time only* and sorts out what is a real problem from what is unrealistic worry. It involves examining what you can control versus what you can't, what you can do something about versus what you can do nothing about. And it helps you make arrangements for when it would be a good idea to worry again.

When people face troubling circumstances, they worry. Most anyone would. This method turns worrying into a combination of planning and thought-stopping for situations that are serious and have a measure of ambiguity, such as when you are undergoing medical treatment, experiencing legal trouble, or waiting to hear whether you passed the state bar exam.

Here is the process:

1. Start by listing all the things you could be worried about. Dissect your problem.
2. Then, do anything that must be done at this time and do not delay. Make phone calls, talk to someone, write or make something, repair, clean, or take any action that will improve the situation.
3. Sometimes taking action is only necessary *if the problem should occur.* In that case, make a plan for "what if it occurs?"
4. Ask yourself: "Is there anything else I need to worry about?" Your brain needs to hear a "no." If you say yes, you need to redo steps 1–3.
4. Set a time when it will be necessary to think about the worry again, and write it down somewhere: "If x happens, then I will do y. But if x does not happen, the next time I will review this worry is on March 15." (Note this on your calendar: "Worry about x.")
5. Whenever the worry pops up again, declare, "Stop! I already worried!" and use thought replacement techniques from Chapter 8.

Let's look at an example of how this works. Cornell had high blood pressure. He was worried about the side effects of medication, and he also worried about the possibility of a stroke or other medical complications. Figure 9.5 shows how he set up Worry Well and Only Once.

Now make your own Worry Well and Only Once plan by filling out the following diagram.

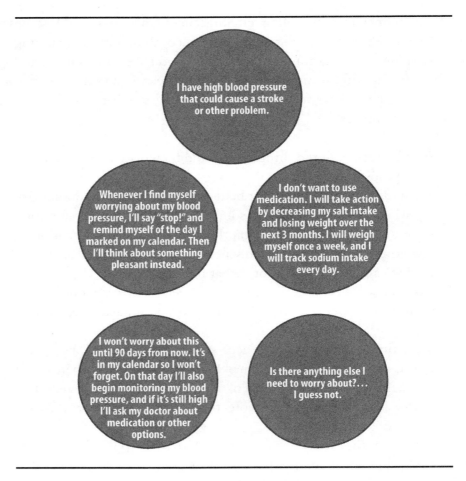

Figure 9.5 Worry Well and Only Once

DITCH YOUR DREAD

The sensation of dread can *precede* the thought that there is something to feel dreadful about. Sometimes this is referred to as "free-floating" anxiety, but it can be recognized by the pit-of-the-stomach unease that all people associate with dread. The circle of dread is shown in Figure 9.6.

If you feel dread, this method is going to be of considerable use to you. But be forewarned: It requires a leap of faith—*you must believe that dread can precede worry and be present for no good reason.* Although worry can indeed make you full of dread, for many with generalized anxiety, it is dread that creates the worry. The

All the things I'm worried about:	• _____ • _____ • _____ • _____ • _____ • _____
What do I need to do right now?	• _____ • _____ • _____ • _____ • _____
What might happen later that I must respond to, and what will I do then?	• _____ • _____ • _____ • _____
Is there anything else I need to worry about?	YES (repeat steps 1–3) NO (go to next step)
When am I going to worry again?	Date and time: _____
When the worry pops up, say: "Stop! I already worried!" Then do thought replacement.	My thought replacements: _____

sensation of doom is an outcome of the neurobiology of anxiety. But it's simple to get rid of.

1. The first step for people who have dread is to come to believe that they will not fail to notice a real problem. Do you have the ability to *recognize* a problem?

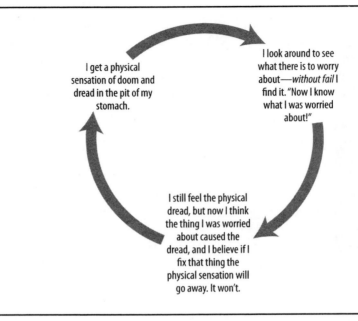

Figure 9.6 The Circle of Dread

2. Next, *notice* the dread. Do not ask what the reason for the dread is; rather, ask, "Is this sensation dread?"
3. Then, find a way to relieve the sensation:
    o *Through diaphragmatic breathing.* With just a minute to breathe and engage in muscle relaxation, the body can relax and begin to let go of the dread at the physical level. (See Chapters 4 and 6 for these techniques.)
    o *Through thought-stopping and thought replacement.* Say to yourself: "Stop! I will not fail to notice a real problem." Then immediately use a thought replacement.

The following statements will help you ditch your dread. On an index card, write down the one that most appeals to you and then carry the card with you.

- A feeling is just a feeling.
- Dread does not need a reason. I will not go on scan mode to find one.

> You will not fail to notice a real problem that needs a solution.

- Breathe, distract.
- I will not fail to notice a real problem. I don't have to look for one.

CLEAR YOUR MIND

Do you feel your mind jumping around or find it hard to stop it from running down a track? Do you need to:

- Get everything off your mind to focus on something important, like studying for a test or writing a report for work?
- Clear away tangled thoughts to think clearly about something?
- Empty your mind to rest?
- Leave work behind to enjoy time off or come into the house ready to be home?

If this is what you need, Clear Your Mind is the method you need. There is more than one version, but all are simple.

The "Container" Version

This version of the method is included on the CD that accompanies this workbook, on Track 7, "Contain Your Worry." Basically, it goes like this:

1. Imagine a container sitting in front of you. It is container that can hold all your concerns. The container is open and ready to receive whatever you want to put into it.
2. Now, think about (but don't mull over) all the things that are pressing on your awareness or asking for your attention. Anything—good or bad, big or small—can go into the container. Give each thing a name.
3. When everything has been named and put in the container, place the lid on the container and set the container aside.
4. If the next thing you want to do is sleep, invite a peaceful thought into your mind.
5. If you want to focus on something, invite into your mind thoughts about what your focus is.

Other Versions

Some people are not fond of the container imagery, and if that is the case for you, or if you just want more than one way to clear your mind, here are other ways to use this method:

- *The list.* Write down your thoughts in the form of a list. Be very brief. Use one or two words to list those things that occupy your thoughts. Then put the list in a drawer, briefcase, or other place where it will literally be out of sight (and out of mind.)
- *The God Box.* This version comes from Al-Anon. The "God Box" is used to hold slips of paper, each of which have a thought that is to be turned over to God.
- *Pictures in a backpack.* This version works best with children. They can write or draw a picture of their thoughts or worries and put it into a worry box, a worry file, or worry backpack that a counselor or teacher keeps for them. With that adult, they can periodically open the backpack and see what is in it. They will learn that worry passes, and if bad things happened, they lived through them and coped.
- *Worry dolls.* There are small dolls in a box or bag from Guatemala that can be purchased from global marketers or import stores. The legend is that a person can hand the concerns or worries of life over to the dolls and the dolls will take the worries away. The lid is literally put on the box so that the dolls can carry the worry away and ready themselves for the next batch of worries.

People of any age can use the Clearing the Mind method, and people of all ages need to use it. All of us have times when we have to make a transition and need a clear mind to walk into the new situation. We have times when we need to focus exclusively on one thing for school or work. Or we might want to leave work behind to enjoy time with our family or friends. We have times when it is hard to turn off our thoughts in order to fall asleep. Regardless of which Clear the Mind method you use, you will get control of runaway thoughts.

S.I.M.P.L.E. PLAN TO CONTAIN WORRY

This chapter has presented several ideas to begin containing your worry. Some will seem more like what you need than others. Pick one idea that seems best for you and work out a S.I.M.P.L.E. plan to begin using it.

S.I.M.P.L.E. Plan to Contain Worry

S: What is the *symptom* or *situation?* _____
_____
_____

I: What is the *impact* on my life? _____
_____
_____

M: What *method* am I trying? _____
_____
_____

P: *Practice* plan. _____
_____
_____

L: *Lifework.* _____
_____
_____

E: *Evaluate.* _____
_____
_____

A FINAL WORD

These ways to contain your worry all have an ultimate goal of "turning it off"— of giving your worried mind a chance to rest and to calm down that "hot" worry activity in your brain. If you are persistent and consistent in using these methods, your brain will calm down and generate less worry. Control of your anxious mind is won slowly, purposefully, and persistently. If you are willing to put in effort, the payoff will be a calmer, quieter, less anxiety-generating brain.

TEN

Technique #8: Talk Yourself Into Changing Behavior

Fear of fear is a dominant behavior changer when you suffer panic or social anxiety disorder. If you've had a panic attack while in a crowded supermarket, for example, you probably now fear going to the supermarket at busy times. If you've found yourself stammering at company meetings, you probably now fear future company meetings. This fear of feeling afraid leads you to avoid those situations. Unfortunately, this kind of avoidance also begins to curtail your freedom in increasingly severe ways. And it keeps you from developing skills to deal with discomfort and to try doing things in a different way.

Much of the impact of fear lies in the way you think about it, and the way you think about fear has to do with your self-talk—the running dialogue you have with yourself in your head. By changing your self-talk, you can begin changing your avoidance behavior. This technique reflects how changing the mind and changing behavior are intimately linked.

Let's start by looking at avoidance behavior—the biggest challenge for people with anxiety, especially panic and social anxiety.

ASSESS YOUR AVOIDANCE

Avoidance of certain places and situations may begin at a fairly low level—for example, if you had a panic attack during a theater performance, you may avoid going to future theater performances, which may not be a terribly big sacrifice in the broad scheme of things. But avoidance behaviors tend to escalate, and soon you're avoiding not only theater performances but also cinema complexes, sports stadiums, and even the school auditorium where your daughter is having her first piano recital.

Are Avoidance Behaviors Beginning to Impinge on Your Life?
Check the following questions that you can answer "yes" to:

☐ Do you stay away from places where you might have a panic attack?
☐ When you go into a new setting, do you check how you can escape?
☐ Do you avoid television shows or news reports about topics that raise your anxiety?
☐ Do you avoid thinking about topics that make you feel anxious?
☐ Do you make an effort to avoid being observed or being the center of attention?
☐ Do you worry ahead of time about what a new situation will be like and sometimes go to check it out ahead of time to reduce your anxiety?

If you checked "yes" for even one of these questions, you will want to specifically identify your arenas of avoiding. Make a list of situations, places, or interactions with others that you have avoided. Here are some examples of common things people avoid:

• Going into large lecture classes at college
• Traveling by air
• Driving on a limited-access highway
• Going to the grocery store during the day
• Speaking in class or at a meeting
• Meeting new people (at work, at a meeting, at a party)

ASSESS YOUR INTENSITY OF FEAR

Now that you have your list of situations, places, or interactions with others that you have avoided, you're going to chart the level of fear each of those situations produces on a scale from 1 to 10, with 1 being low and 10 being high. Figure 10.1 illustrates how to do this. The left-hand column rates the level of fear you experienced during the times you have actually been in that situation. The middle column rates the level of fear you experience when you anticipate being in

The 10 Best-Ever Anxiety Management Techniques Workbook

that situation again. The right-hand column rates your level of fear after you've avoided the situation.

In the example shown in Figure 10.1, the situation was "driving over a bridge." The actual times the person had driven over a bridge produced a high level of fear, so she colored in the boxes through the number 10. The morning she had to drive to a location that required crossing a bridge, her fear was at a very high 9. When she decided, halfway there, to cancel the trip so she wouldn't have to cross the bridge, her fear dropped to a 2.

A blank chart for you to fill out follows Figure 10.1.

How much did your level of fear drop after you'd avoided the situation? You probably felt a lot of relief! This shows why avoidance is such a tempting way to deal with situations that make you anxious.

My experience is that when the intensity of your anticipatory fear is between 5 and 7, you will avoid the situation *except when* the need to face it is

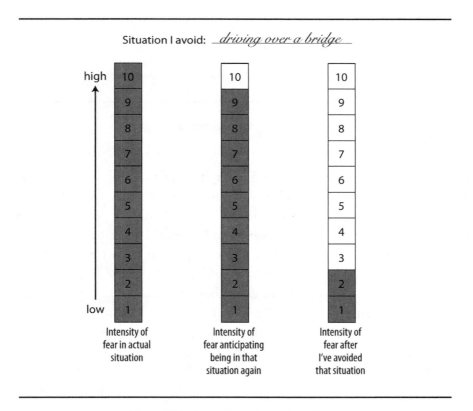

Figure 10.1 Assess Your Intensity of Fear

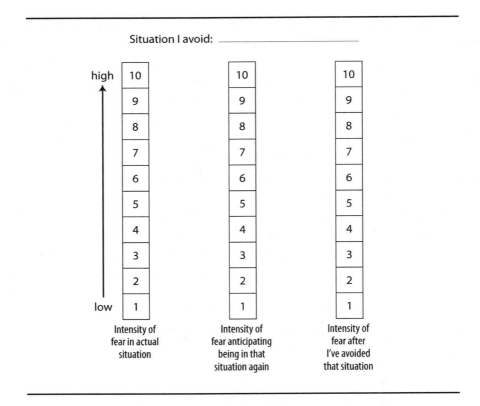

Situation I avoid: _____

high 10   10   10
      9   9   9
      8   8   8
      7   7   7
      6   6   6
      5   5   5
      4   4   4
      3   3   3
      2   2   2
low   1   1   1

Intensity of   Intensity of   Intensity of
fear in actual   fear anticipating   fear after
situation   being in that   I've avoided
                    situation again   that situation

Figure 10.1 Continued

stronger. For example, a woman who is terrified of walking into an emergency room because she's afraid of seeing someone bleeding may force herself to go despite her fear if her child needs emergency care. When the intensity of anticipatory fear goes to 8 or above, people tend to avoid the situation even if the consequences are very negative. I've had clients who have canceled important medical appointments, have walked off airplanes after they have boarded, and have dropped out of college classes even though it meant losing their financial aid and course credit.

If you want to learn how to stop avoiding, the first step will be decreasing fear and increasing motivation. The way to do this is by changing your self-talk and learning to tolerate your feelings without fear of them. Track 8 on the CD, "Managing Uncomfortable Sensations," is a place to start that process. Once you've decreased your fear and increased your motivation, you can begin learn-ing the skills you need—skills to reduce anxiety and skills to do the activities that frighten you.

ASSESS YOUR SELF-TALK

Again, self-talk is the running dialogue you have with yourself in your head. It's when you argue both sides of a problem with yourself, and it includes hearing in your mind the voice of a parent, coach, or acquaintance.

All too often the self-talk we engage in expresses criticism and doubt. "Should I try to talk to that attractive woman at the end of the bar? I guess not—I'm sure she wouldn't be interested in me, and I'd probably say something dumb." "Should I accept my friend's invitation to go to the baseball game? The last time I was in a stadium, I panicked, and I'll probably panic again. I guess I should tell him I can't go."

Is Your Self-Talk a Problem?

Check the following questions that you can answer "yes" to:

☐ I tell myself that I will make a fool of myself if I try something new.
☐ I tell myself that people will not like me.
☐ I tell myself that no one else answers questions incorrectly or stumbles when trying to explain things in meetings or classrooms.
☐ I tell myself that I will not be able to stand it if I blush or get embarrassed and others notice it.
☐ I tell myself people will not notice if I don't show up or participate, so it's okay if I don't go to the event.
☐ I tell myself that I will feel scared and I can't stand feeling scared.

If you checked "yes" to 2 or more of these questions, you need to learn how to begin changing your negative self-talk.

Negative inner dialogue increases fear and anxiety and causes us to antici-pate failure and rejection, thus preventing us from taking action that would be positive for us. The biggest problem with self-talk, especially when we do not realize we are doing it, is that it has the ring of truth. *You tend to believe what you say to yourself.*

And self-talk is predictive. If you tell yourself that something is going to be scary, chances are excellent that you will perceive it as scary. Then the emotional part of your brain will think "this is scary!" and reinforce your negative self-talk as *true*. Your brain will then go on to warn you that every similar situation will be scary, and thus a self-fulfilling prophecy about social fear or panic is born.

On the positive side, however, if you deliberately make *positive* self-statements, you may well start to believe them! That is the goal of this technique.

IS AVOIDANCE INTERFERING WITH YOUR GOALS?

Changing behavior starts with the conviction that behavior change is necessary. Is your avoidance behavior getting in the way of your goals? What do you want? To be able to go on a job interview? To be able to participate in class? To speak up at a meeting or point out your successes as your peers do? Knowing what you have to gain by facing fear or anxiety is the first step to sticking with a plan for change. And writing it down reinforces that knowledge. So take a moment here to write down your goals. What will you do if you have less anxiety? What quality of life are you seeking? What changes in relationships will occur if you feel better? Figure 10.2 is an example.

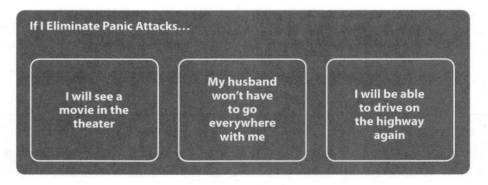

Figure 10.2 What Will I Get When I Get Rid Of Anxiety?

The 10 Best-Ever Anxiety Management Techniques Workbook

Now fill in your own.

Goal:

Outcome: _____   Outcome: _____   Outcome: _____
_____   _____   _____
_____   _____   _____
_____   _____   _____
_____   _____   _____
_____   _____   _____

When you can see what your goals are, it is time to look at what is stopping you. How is your self-talk interfering with getting rid of anxiety? If you have anxiety, you have developed some beliefs about your condition. You may believe it is impossible to control, or you may believe that panicking means you are going crazy. Those beliefs get in your way.

GET EDUCATED ABOUT ANXIETY: THE NECESSARY PRECURSOR TO CHANGE

It's important to remember that anxiety is a protective response. Your brain and body try to protect you by warning you of possible risks. For example, if you're hiking on a mountain trail and suddenly come face-to-face with a bear, you're probably going to feel very anxious. Your heart rate will jump, and your brain will tell you, "Run! You're not capable of fighting off this bear!" That response works to keep you safe much of the time.

The problem is when your brain and body send out "Danger! Warning!" signs when the situation isn't actually risky. Your brain might warn you, for instance, to stay away from a dinner party you've been invited to because you might embarrass yourself. Or that you're not competent to handle the anxiety you might feel being in a crowded theater. Or that your daughter has been in a terrible car accident when she's a few minutes late getting home from school. You have to learn to talk back to that warning. Changing self-talk will help you:

- Learn to tolerate uncomfortable sensations as merely uncomfortable, not awful

- Take control of negative self-talk and eliminate it
- Act in direct opposition to false beliefs you hold about your competence
- Develop confidence that you can control fear and stop avoiding life

Basic Ideas to Master

Before you begin looking at ways to change your negative self-talk, learn and remember the following basic ideas about anxiety and how to manage it:

- Panic, worry, and social fears can be changed by changing thoughts and behaviors.
- Social anxiety is not specifically fear of danger, but rather fear of exposure (i.e., the fear that others will observe you looking embarrassed). Blushing, sweating, and shaking are autonomic responses to being exposed. The more you tell yourself you will be humiliated, the greater the risk of these symptoms.
- Changing self-talk and beliefs is a key component of changing behavior. Beliefs drive action.
- Practicing new behavior is the ultimate way to get rid of fear.

FIND AND CHANGE YOUR SELF-TALK

Hint: In order to counter negative thoughts you must identify them first. Listen carefully to the way you talk to yourself!

The impact of beliefs about yourself, the world, and other people can be easily seen in choices you make and are revealed in your self-talk. Every small thought that creates anxiety must be identified and corrected. What are some ways to find out what you are saying to yourself?

Ask Yourself "So What?"

People can be unaware of how they talk to themselves in self-sabotaging ways. To hear your own voice, start out by being a detective in your own life. As you go through experiences, try to objectively notice exactly what happens and what you are saying to yourself. Write down everything so you don't overlook any important details. Copy down the following questions on an index card (or put them in your smartphone) and carry it with you at all times:

1. Notice: Where am I and what am I doing?
2. Notice: What are my anxiety symptoms and how bad are they?
3. Ask yourself: "*So what* if I have these symptoms?"

Your answer to this last question will reveal your negative inner dialogue or self-talk. Take a look at Figure 10.3.

Where am I and what am I doing?
- I am in a meeting.
- My turn to speak is coming soon.
- People are looking at me.

What are my symptoms and how bad are they?
- My heart is racing, my face is probably red, and my hands are shaking visibly.
- They are pretty bad: about a 7 out of 10.

So what if I look nervous and they notice?
- I will look stupid.
- I will feel humiliated and I hate that feeling.

Figure 10.3 Finding Your Self-Talk

Now identify a specific situation you find yourself in and fill out the blank form.

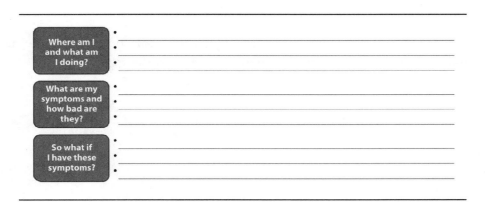

Where am I and what am I doing?
- _____
- _____
- _____

What are my symptoms and how bad are they?
- _____
- _____
- _____

So what if I have these symptoms?
- _____
- _____
- _____

Counter Negative Self-Talk

Once you know what you are telling yourself, you have to replace it. There are a couple of good methods to do this, one of which is countering negative statements by replacing them with opposites. In this method you will identify each part of an activity or situation that you want to do and then construct a list of negative thoughts you have about that specific goal. The next step is to create replacement thoughts. Then, every time you engage in the negative self-talk, you will read or say the replacement thought *immediately*. This will allow you to deliberately override your negativity and lay the groundwork for willingness to change behavior.

Figure 10.4 shows how this worked for Guy, a 22-year-old who wanted to go back to college after he had dropped out due to anxiety. He knew he had the intelligence to go to school, and it bothered him that he was working in a gas station when he could be in school. He listed his goals and then noted the negative self-talk that was interfering with doing what he wanted to do. Finally, he planned replacement thoughts and wrote them into the third column of this chart.

This was Guy's list of goals:

- I want to start school in 6 weeks.
- I want to talk to the admissions office about getting all my other credits accepted.
- I want to be able to talk to other students about the classes.
- I want to attend every class, and not leave at any time due to nervousness.
- I want to finish school completely in 2½ years.

Now create your own three-column table, with goals on the left, negative thoughts in the middle, and replacement thoughts on the right.

Goals, Actions, Intentions	First Thought (negative self-talk)	Opposite of First Thought (positive replacement thought)
Start school in 6 weeks	I may not be able to meet that timeline. I always miss deadlines.	I have filled out applications before and I know I have time to do this. I will use my support system to encourage me.
Talk to admissions about getting credits accepted	I don't know where to go and I don't know whom to talk to there. It might not even be worth it—I bet they won't transfer credits from the junior college.	I can call ahead to get the information about whom to see and where to go. Other students figure it out, so I can too. I can't know what they will accept if I don't ask. It is worth it financially to make this effort, even if I don't like it.
Talk to other students	I will make a fool of myself. I am no good at talking to strangers.	Everyone in the class will be strangers to each other. Talking about class does not require me to be witty or tell jokes—just to talk, which I can do.
Attend every class and not leave because I am nervous	I have always run out of class.	Even if I am nervous, I can stay. I have practiced skills to stay.
Finish school completely in 2 1/2 years	I will never finish school. I don't think I have ever stayed long enough to get enough credits.	Things are different today. I have a goal, and I can stay in school even if it is hard.

Figure 10.4 Planning Replacement Thoughts for Negative Self-Talk

Goals, Actions, Intentions	First Thought (negative self-talk)	Opposite of First Thought (positive replacement thought)

Recite Affirmations

It is no surprise that self-talk contributes to failure to do and be what we want. People often fail because they believe they will fail. If you have anxiety, you fail in advance by avoiding anything that seems too tough. When we say to ourselves that we will be too frightened or embarrassed if we try, we set ourselves up for failure. Our chances of success are much better if we imagine ourselves succeeding, see ourselves doing something right. By affirming what we want to be true (about our lives, our situations, our character, our attitudes, and so on) we create the conditions for that truth.

Affirmations are a way to form thoughts that counteract negative self-talk. An affirmation is a positive statement about yourself, said aloud it as if it is already true. The idea behind affirmations is that you will more readily create the conditions for what you desire if you think and speak it aloud. For example, if you want to become more comfortable talking at meetings, an affirmation you might say would be, "I am confident and competent when I express myself at staff meetings." You say the affirmation as if the attitude and action is true right now.

Hint: For affirmations to be helpful, they must be believable and possible.

For affirmations to be helpful, they must be believable and possible. Telling yourself "I am fully capable of jumping off the high dive" when you don't even know how to swim certainly won't do you any good! First you need to learn to swim—or gain skills in public speaking if that's your fear, or learn the new computer software at work if you're anxious about your job performance. Again, affirmations are only useful to combat negative self-talk when they are actually believable and possible.

What reality do you want to create? Do you want to fly in an airplane? Do you want to be comfortable dating? Do you want to audition for the band or go on a job interview? Figure out what you want, and then form the right phrase. Try writing an affirmation for yourself about something you want. Figure 10.5 shows an example.

CHANGE THE FILTERS ON EXPERIENCE

You know that your past performance is the best predictor of your future performance. That fact might cause distress if you believe you cannot change your panic or social anxieties. So you will want to develop new expectations about

---

My Affirmation

What I want: I want to complete this workbook and feel less anxious when I am meeting new people.

I affirm: I am competent to meet and greet new people and confident that I can do it without fear.

Figure 10.5 My Affirmation

the future. In Chapter 12 you will look carefully at how to prepare and practice new actions so you feel comfortable doing them. But first, you must change your thinking about your ability to change behavior. To believe you really can accomplish behavior change, you must change your "filters" on your experiences.

The fact is, *you have probably succeeded far more often than you have failed*. But if you are like many people with panic or social anxiety, you tend to see only the times when you fled a room feeling like you were going to suffocate, or remember only the times when you became embarrassed. You obsess about wrong answers you gave at school, the bad throws in the game, or the times you froze and did not speak when you should have. If you have generalized anxiety, you may remember only the times when your dread *did* precede something bad happening—even though 99 times out of 100 nothing terrible came to pass and your dread was just a false alarm.

When you've had a negative experience, you start to filter new experiences through a lens of expecting the same bad outcome. You go on the lookout for bad experiences and do not notice positive ones. Worse, you make inaccurate generalizations about your experiences: "I panicked the last time I drove on the highway, so I will obviously panic *whenever* I drive on the highway." People with social fear expect to be humiliated or expect themselves to be unassertive, ignored, or flustered. They stop seeing the moments when other people responded warmly to them or when they succeeded socially. And people with generalized anxiety fail to notice all the times their dread proved to be a false alarm. All of this seems to prove the self-talk true.

In these cases, self-talk is not accurate. It reflects specific kinds of cognitive errors that are common to anxiety. The problem is that these mental errors go unchallenged because you begin avoiding new situations that could contradict them.

Figure 10.6 illustrates some common cognitive errors, along with examples of each.

Some additional cognitive errors you may recognize include:

- Underestimating your capacity to tolerate negative experience. You may believe you cannot handle anxious feelings or believe you cannot tolerate having something go wrong. (In fact, however, you would not be doing this workbook if you had not tolerated plenty of negative experiences already!)

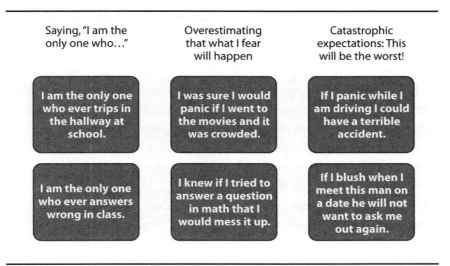

Saying, "I am the only one who…"	Overestimating that what I fear will happen	Catastrophic expectations: This will be the worst!
I am the only one who ever trips in the hallway at school.	I was sure I would panic if I went to the movies and it was crowded.	If I panic while I am driving I could have a terrible accident.
I am the only one who ever answers wrong in class.	I knew if I tried to answer a question in math that I would mess it up.	If I blush when I meet this man on a date he will not want to ask me out again.

Figure 10.6 Cognitive Errors You May Recognize

- Believing you do not have control over how you feel.
- Believing you do not have control over any part of the outcome of situations; believing you will inevitably feel rejected or embarrassed if others notice you.

Now fill in the following diagram with your own examples of these cognitive errors. You can add any other types of cognitive errors you may make, too.

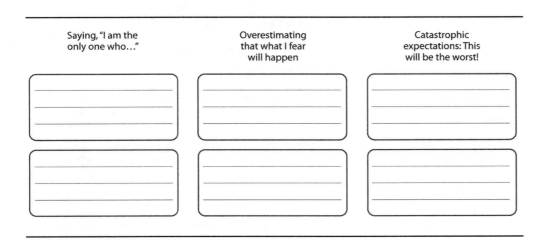

Correcting cognitive errors starts with a search for situations that disprove these beliefs. Look at the diagram you just filled out, and list times the situations did not have the outcome you feared.

- Have there been times when you did *not* experience rejection or humiliation? (An important note here: Even though you might have felt embarrassed, did others *actually* humiliate you? Saying that the other person probably was *thinking* negative thoughts doesn't count!)
- Have there been times when you did *not* panic in a crowded room, on an airplane, while driving, etc.?
- Have there been times when nothing bad ended up happening even though you were feeling a sense of dread?

Write down as many of these positive situations as you can—actually writing them down will help you remember them. Figure 10.7 is an example of how to notice and write down a change in your filter. A blank diagram for you to fill out follows it.

Figure 10.7 Changing Your Filter

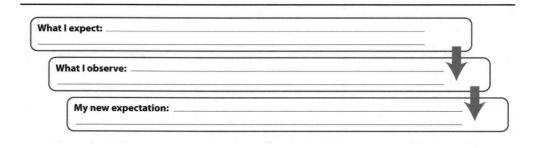

The 10 Best-Ever Anxiety Management Techniques Workbook

Now keep up this search for positives as a regular part of countering your negative self-talk. Unlearning a lifetime of negative filtering takes some time!

S.I.M.P.L.E. PLAN TO TALK YOURSELF INTO CHANGING BEHAVIOR

It is very important that you make a commitment to listening to yourself and changing the way you talk to yourself. Was there anything in this chapter that spoke to you about the way you speak to yourself? Identify a place to start, and make a plan to carry out the change. Remember that consistently changing inner dialogue will change your behavior automatically.

S.I.M.P.L.E. Plan to Talk Yourself Into Changing Behavior

S: What is the *symptom* or *situation?* _____
_____
_____

I: What is the *impact* on my life? _____
_____
_____

M: What *method* am I trying? _____
_____
_____

P: *Practice* plan. _____
_____
_____

L: *Lifework.* _____
_____
_____

E: *Evaluate.* _____
_____
_____

A FINAL WORD

Many skills must be learned and interwoven for the best success in recovering from any anxiety problem. Changing your inner dialogue takes time. People who have not exercised for years cannot get up and run a marathon tomorrow. No one would expect them to. They would need to start with a short walk, practice it, repeat it, and extend it to be longer and faster before they could ever expect to make a long run. Every small step of progress is necessary. This is true of changing anxious behavior by changing self-talk, too. Starting with the change of self-talk is like taking walks before getting to the run that prepares you for the marathon.

PART IV

Managing Anxious Behavior

ELEVEN

Technique #9: Control TMA
(Too Much Activity)

The methods in this technique are for people who consider themselves high-drive. This type of personality is usually evident in childhood, and although being energetic isn't a problem in itself, as people get older and busier their high-drive style can easily turn into generalized anxiety.

Too much activity (TMA) serves a purpose. High activity *diminishes* anxiety in the person whose brain is set up with this energy. But high-drive people present an anxiety dilemma: They get anxious when they're *not* actively doing something, either mentally or physically, and they get anxious because they typically create *too much* to do.

If you have TMA, you probably feel agitated when you hold still, especially when you have not planned how to use down time, and your feelings of anxiety may escalate rapidly. Your response to this may then be to get very busy and try to ignore the sense of anxiety.

You are probably wondering, "What in the world could be wrong with being a high-drive, productive person?" You don't want to give up your level of productivity. You just want to give up the worrying and general feeling of anxiety that permeates your life. Here is the good news. As you assess yourself and look at methods to diminish anxiety, your energy will be put to good use when you direct it to mastering anxiety.

ASSESS YOUR TMA

Do you suffer from TMA? If you do, you may not recognize it, but the people around you certainly do! Do people often say to you, "I don't know how you get so much done!" or "Where do you get the energy to do that?" or "Don't you ever sleep?" or "How can you take this on when you have so much else to do?" If you hear those kinds of questions, read on: You could be a candidate for TMA.

Do You Suffer from TMA?

For each of the following items, rate yourself on a scale of 1 to 5, with 1 being "not like you" and 5 being "very like you."

_____ Getting unexpected free time can *raise* my anxiety, especially if I have no warning.

_____ I feel as if something is wrong if I am not being productive.

_____ My spouse or partner complains that I never sit down.

_____ I am secretly proud of how much I get done.

_____ Efficiency is very important to me.

_____ I become very impatient when something slows down my progress.

_____ I get irritated when other people do something for me or for my work that I could have done and would have done better.

_____ I feel stuck or frozen when my plans are disrupted.

_____ I have trouble letting other people take over part of my work, whether it is at my job or in preparation for a social event (e.g., letting someone else grill the hamburgers at dinner).

_____ I often find that I spend energy on something that is important to me, but I do not do what is important to people who matter to me.

Score _____

10–20 points = You do not have to worry about TMA or its impact on anxiety.

21–30 points = Pay attention to your high drive. You are on your way to being out of balance and developing anxiety from TMA.

31–40 points = TMA is becoming excessive and it is imperative to start taking control of your activities. Your anxiety is generated or made much worse by TMA.

40–50 points = TMA is creating serious problems and your anxiety may be intense. Be on the lookout for stress-related health and emotional problems—you are on your way to burnout.

TMA AND STUDENTS

I see many young people in high school and college who already qualify for the TMA label. These are students building impressive resumes for college and winning numerous awards for athletics, arts, or academic achievements. Their parents may be too pleased with their success to realize there is a problem brewing.

If you are in high school or college and are feeling anxious, see if TMA is making your anxiety worse.

Are You a Student Who Suffers from TMA?

For each of the following items, rate yourself on a scale of 1 to 5, with 1 being "not like you" and 5 being "very like you."

_____ Getting unexpected free time can *raise* my anxiety, especially if I have no plan for what to do with the time.

_____ I feel as if something is wrong if I am not at an activity or doing homework.

_____ I can only relax if I am playing video games or doing something equally absorbing.

_____ I don't talk about my good grades or successes with peers.

_____ I get very upset if I forget assignments or get a bad grade.

_____ Any bad grade makes me worry that I will fail the course (and a C would be a failure!).

_____ I get irritated when I am forced to work with a group of students because I end up doing it all or suffer because of their bad work.

_____ I feel stuck or frozen when my plans are disrupted.

_____ I feel the need to explain at length any poor performance in a non-classroom activity, especially if other people notice it.

_____ I repeatedly check with teachers, coaches, or faculty advisors to make sure I know their expectations.

Score _____

10–20 points = You do not have to worry about TMA or its impact on anxiety.

21–30 points = Pay attention to your high drive. You are on your way to being out of balance and developing anxiety from TMA.

31–40 points = TMA is going to disrupt social relationships. Your anxiety is generated or made much worse by TMA.

40–50 points = TMA is creating serious problems and you may be feeling the impact on your self-esteem and social life. Be on the lookout for stress-related health and emotional problems—you are on your way to burnout.

CONTROL TMA

One of highest-drive people I ever met was a woman I admire very much for her successes. She was also, sadly, one of the most miserably anxious people I've treated in my practice. Darla was a CPA running her own business. She also managed to be at every activity her children participated in, spearheaded the local high-school fundraisers, and was active in a major community volunteer organization. She was felled by anxiety when she broke her ankle and no longer had the mobility to maintain her active lifestyle. She was supposed to take 6 weeks off—by week 3 she was so consumed by worry that she could no longer sleep. Her previous level of activity had discharged her anxiety, and being forced to remain still and stop her work seriously intensified her anxiety.

This holds true for many people with TMA. They will benefit on many levels by addressing this brain-based energy and the anxiety that often accompanies it. They can start by relaxing their typically tense bodies. Track 9 on the CD, "Tense and Release Progressive Muscle Relaxation," is a terrific way to change "uptight" bodies that occur with TMA.

Plan for Dreaded, Unexpected "Free" Time

This is a brief strategy but genuinely helpful to the overdriven TMA person. Life always produces unexpected times when people have to hold still in one way or another. Appointments get canceled, people don't show up, airline flights are delayed, social events are postponed. If you have TMA, you probably find it especially challenging to hold still unexpectedly. It's as if you get "brain freeze" about what to do next. You feel that you have to choose the most important, useful thing—even if it's just a way to relax or do something nice for yourself. For example, if your son calls to say he is staying at the neighbor's for dinner, you spend the whole time he is gone deciding if it would be better to get a manicure or take a bath. Worried about not making the best choice about what to do with this unexpected free time, you get anxious.

Even a snow day for the TMA student can produce a brain freeze about what to do. A particularly talented senior in high school told me she "lost an entire weekend" when a drama activity was canceled due to inclement weather. She slept late, watched movies, and drank coffee with friends. Toward the end of the weekend, she became upset when she realized she could have been scrap-booking the pictures from the last show she was in—something she'd told herself would be a good idea if she ever had time. She bemoaned, "Now I don't know when I will ever have time again to get that done!" She definitely overestimated the importance of the task and underestimated the value of just relaxing.

The "if I ever have the time" list is a great way to relieve this anxiety. Whenever you say, "If I ever have the time, I want to _____," add that activity to the list, and keep the list handy. The activities you list can include anything at all—calling a friend, building shelves in the garage, baking bread, taking a bath. *Anything* can go on this list. Try it now. Look around your home or office and see if you can find five things you will do if you ever have the time.

1. _____
2. _____
3. _____
4. _____
5. _____

Now:

1. For each item, note how long it will take.
2. Carry the list with you, and whenever faced with dreaded un-expected "free" time, select an activity from the list that fits the available time. (Because you're already certain that you want to do it, you will be able to select something quickly, and your anxiety about picking will be relieved.)
3. As you complete tasks, cross them off and keep adding new "if I ever have time" items when you think of them. This is *very* satis-fying for people with TMA.

Your list might look something like that pictured in Figure 11.1.

If I Ever Have the Time . . .

1. _I will organize those pictures into a book on Shutterfly (2 hours)_

2. _I will finally put that diploma into a frame (15 minutes—or 45 if I have to buy the frame)_

3. _I want to go to that new shop with art supplies and see what it has (30-60 minutes)_

4. _I will go through my files and throw away notes and papers I do not need (60 minutes)_

5. _I will put shelves up in the garage and stack things on them (6 hours)_

Figure 11.1 If I Ever Have the Time . . .

Identify and Counter Perfectionism

When people who are anxious seem like perfectionists, they often do not see themselves as such. They do not feel wedded to making everything perfect, as if order and correctness were goals in themselves. Rather, perfectionism for them is a way to ward off anxiety, even if they don't realize it. The underlying belief is: "If I do enough, carefully enough, then I will never make mistakes and I won't have to worry." And this works well—until the person makes a mistake. Then he or she has to raise the bar on being better, more careful, and more thorough. And this, of course, reinforces the perfectionism.

You may not realize your anxiety will come back no matter how hard you work. You already know that people want you to work hard—after all, you get results! But you may fear that if you ever let down your perfectionist guard, things will *completely* fall apart and be *absolutely*, *terribly* wrong, and others will blame you *entirely*. (Note the extreme language here—"completely," "entirely." It's the way the thought process goes.) In other words, you believe that *everyone* sees your mistakes as intolerable and as proof of your unworthiness. The person with TMA perfectionism often sees no way out.

Identify Perfectionism

To get a better sense of how perfectionism plays a role in your personal life, write down answers to the following questions.

1. I have a strong sense of *personal* responsibility for the outcome of work, social, or family activities, especially when other people could be reasonably expected to do some of the work. How do I show that? _____

   _____

   _____

   _____

   _____

   _____

2. I hear myself use extreme words like "always," "never," and "this is terrible," and I see the consequences of mistakes as being extreme (failure, ruin, etc.). Here are some examples: _____

   _____

_____
_____
_____
_____
_____

3. I am very watchful about details, and I think it is a good idea. Here are the ways I am detailed-oriented: _____
_____
_____
_____
_____
_____

4. I cannot always see the difference between "good enough" and "perfect" when it comes to my responsibilities. Here is an example: _____
_____
_____
_____
_____
_____

See the Price of Your Perfectionism

Do any of the following apply to you?

- Have you been blamed (unfairly) for being controlling and not been seen as helpful or careful?
- Have you taken on extra work that no one asked you to do and later felt overworked?
- Do you firmly believe you would have fun if you could only find the time?
- When you are responsible for an activity (such as hosting a party), do you feel a lack of pleasure and fun despite the fact that the activity *should* be fun?
- Do you feel completely exhausted and have no idea how or when you will recover?

- Are you noticing that you feel anxious, even when paying very close attention to details, in one arena of responsibility?

If you answered "yes" to even one of the above, it means your perfectionism is having negative consequences on your life. It's time to work less and figure out another way to let go of anxiety. Pick one of the following and commit to a specific way to try it in the coming week:

> *Hint: Remember the saying "Your urgency does not constitute an emergency for me!"*

- Commit to letting others do a part of what you feel responsible for, even if you believe they won't do it as well.
- Every time you catch yourself using "all/never" language, tell yourself to stop it immediately. Doing this will undermine the idea that perfectionism is possible. A slogan for anxious perfectionists should be: "Perfection is impossible." Follow that slogan with: "If something is impossible, then I have no obligation to try for it."
- Plan for non-perfectionism. Actually planning a non-perfect performance of some responsibilities will work better than noticing accidental imperfection. It won't be quite as anxiety-provoking because you will be doing it on purpose, and you will have made sure you can tolerate the outcome.

Instructions for the perfectionist include:

- Let someone else step up to the plate (e.g., don't agree to mow the lawn just because your kid complains when you ask him to do it, don't agree to babysit at the last minute, don't write that report your colleague is dragging his feet on, don't agree to cover someone else's shift). You may well find that when you hold back someone else will step up. Even if the work doesn't get done, it's not end the world.
- Observe and evaluate how people respond to the imperfect work of others.
- Do not do work others are responsible for. Observe how this affects the attitudes of others and your own anxiety level.
- Finally, plan to not finish some work that you would otherwise have knocked yourself out to do. Miss a deadline by a little bit, or

just don't do something. You may have to get advice on what you can let go, but do it. (Pick something that seems minor in the eyes of others. Some good examples are: Don't go out to buy the right napkins for the party—use paper towels. Ask if you can have a one-day extension on a project—see what the boss or teacher says. Don't prepare the agenda in writing before the staff meeting. These kinds of detail-oriented things that you believe are major are probably going to turn out to be inconsequential most of the time.)

Now commit to doing it:

I will _____

_____

_____

On this date or in this situation _____

_____

Finally, evaluate the outcome:

Did anyone care whether I was perfect? Their names are _____

_____

_____

If something went wrong unexpectedly, how did I and others cope?

_____

_____

_____

Can I tell the difference between the consequential things and inconsequential things? What did I note? _____

_____

This evaluation will help you make future decisions about what you can drop and what is essential.

ACHIEVE THE RIGHT BALANCE

Achieving balance in life results in emotional, physical, and mental wellbeing. People with TMA get out of balance unintentionally. There are times, of course, when it's important to devote more attention to one part of your life. For example, if you're preparing to sell your company, getting your agency ready for inspection, or studying for a final exam, it might be perfectly reasonable to work 12 hours a day for a circumscribed period of time. But shifting back to balanced activity is often a problem for the TMA person, who can easily continue on that work, work, work trajectory even when other aspects of life are also important. How often have you heard someone say, "I know I should exercise and take care of my health, but . . ." or "I know I *should* spend more time with my kids, but . . ." or "I know it would be *better* if I took time for myself every day, but . . ."? These kinds of statements indicate a lack of balance.

> *Hint: Is your life working like a washing machine with one rug in it? Getting the job done, but revolving with a thunk instead of a smooth spin? Add something good to life!*

Keep Track of Your Time

People with TMA can be very, very good at thinking they are sufficiently balanced, even when others in their lives do not see it that way. They need objective evidence. Here's a way to get it.

1. Keep track of what you are doing with your time for at least a week, every day. (If the week is not representative of your normal routine, do it for 2 weeks.)
2. Divide your week into hours, with 15-minute time slots in each day. Fill it in as you go—not at the end of the week—to keep from fooling yourself. See Figure 11.2. (Note that there are 16 hours in the example here, assuming you spend 8 hours sleeping. If that is not the case, add the extra waking hours and record what you do with them.)
3. Now make a list of categories into which your daily activities fit. Include *everything*—personal hygiene, watching television, eating, time with friends, work, and so on. (If you are having trouble getting all your work done in a reasonable amount of time, divide work activities into separate categories in your list—email, phone calls, meetings, paperwork, etc.)

	M	T	W	Th	F	S	S
Hour 1	15 m. bkfst 45 m. shwr						
Hour 2	45 m. commute 15 m. email						
Hour 3	15 m. email 45 m. mtgs						
Hour 4	60 m. mtgs						
Hour 5	30 m. return calls 15 m. talk w/ colleague 15 m. snack						
Hour 6							
Hour 7							
Hour 8							
Hour 9							
Hour 10							
Hour 11							
Hour 12							
Hour 13							
Hour 14							
Hour 15							
Hour 16							

Figure 11.2 Keep Track of Your Time

The 10 Best-Ever Anxiety Management Techniques Workbook

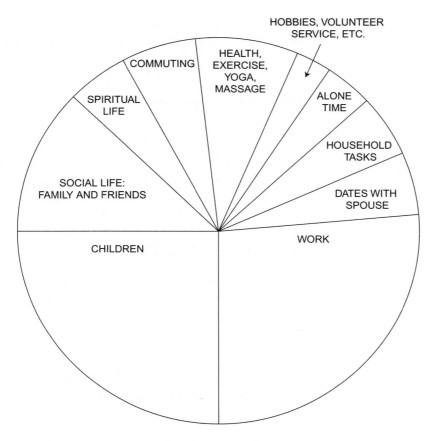

Figure 11.3 Is There Balance in Your Life?

4. Add up the minutes you spent on the activities in each category.
5. Use these totals to create a pie chart showing the amount of time you spend on each category. See Figure 11.3 for an example.

Evaluate How Your Use of Time Fits Your Values

Now that you can see how you are spending your time, does the proportion of it make sense to you? Does it seem off-balance? For example, are you spending more time with family and friends when you want to spend more with your spouse? If so, begin to rebalance your life with this one method: Increase the time you spend on something you want very much to do, and spend less time on something that matters less.

Another exercise to help with this process—especially when you're evaluating just a couple of aspects of your life—is the following "weigh the importance" chart.

Weigh the Importance

Question	Answer
How important is it that I do this task/activity?	
How important are all the things I am *not* doing in order to do this task/activity? What are those things?	

Using Your Values to Make Decisions

If you're having a hard time making a decision in any situation in which you have to make a choice (e.g., whether to take a job, buy a house, go to one school versus another), it's probably because you're not taking your values into consideration. Try the following exercise.

Using My Values to Make a Decision

Identify a situation (e.g., taking a new job, buying a house, going to school).
_____

Make a list of every important aspect of the situation that affects your decision.
_____
_____
_____
_____
_____
_____
_____
_____

Now sort the list according to a hierarchy of what is the most significant. Sometimes it's easy to see what is important, but sometimes it's not so clear. You can clarify your values by comparing one significant item to each of the others on your list. What's the new hierarchy, starting with the most important thing at the top?

The 10 Best-Ever Anxiety Management Techniques Workbook

1. _____
2. _____
3. _____
4. _____
5. _____
6. _____
7. _____
8. _____

Now make a decision. Ask, "Does this decision support the important things in my life?"

REDIRECT TMA TO HAVE SOME FUN

If you have TMA, you are probably overworked and under-relaxed. One client of mine, Betty, described it well. She said she liked to entertain. It was fun for her to plan, cook, and create a party. She also said she didn't remember much about her parties because she was so busy being a nonstop perfect hostess—the "fun" was hearing that her guests enjoyed themselves. Classic TMA—too much work blotted out the fun.

Laughter Is a Good Start

Laughing is a great way to increase good feelings while discharging physical energy. Recreating fun and getting the relief of laughing is serious therapy for the serious person. Ask yourself "what makes me laugh?"

Hint: Belly laughing is as good for your abs as it is for your mood. TMA people like to multitask, so remembering this may increase your desire to laugh!

What Makes Me Laugh?

Make a list of things or activities that make you laugh. Usually these things require little time and little or no money.

1. _____
2. _____
3. _____
4. _____

Now make a plan to do one of those things within the next 7 days.

I will _____

And I will do it with _____

On this day and time _____

Look for "Busy Fun" Opportunities

Because people with TMA don't like to sit still, they often find "busy fun" activities (such as a day of gardening, a 40-mile bike ride, or hitting every garage sale in town on a Saturday morning) more relaxing than activities that are more leisurely (such as a massage or soak in the tub). When choosing busy fun activities, make sure you distinguish between those that are pleasurable to *do* and those that are pleasurable because they give you a sense of *accomplishment* afterward. The goal is to find activities that you enjoy as you actually do them. Ask yourself these questions:

- Was the activity itself pleasurable or unpleasurable?
- When I recall each aspect of the activity, are most of them pleasing?

Hint: Saying "I have to" in front of a fun activity—as in "I have to go to the Bahamas"—is a sure sign of TMA stress. Back off of work, not fun!

TMA AT DIFFERENT AGES AND IN SPECIAL CIRCUMSTANCES

Although TMA is more prevalent in adults in their working years, it can affect people of any age. Following are some guidelines for spotting TMA in children, adolescents, and the elderly. (See the Recommended Reading and Resources section for more information on getting help for these age groups.)

A warning sign for anxiety in children is being serious, tense, and constantly busy. Observe:

- Have parents set up too much activity because of their own anxiety about failing to push a child to explore his or her potential in every way possible?

- Is all of the child's play time organized?
- Is something in the home—such as abuse or a family secret—keeping the child vigilant?
- Are there possible mental-health issues, such as obsessive-compulsive disorder?
- Is the child's anxiety specifically related to his or her social skills?

Adolescents who are constantly tense may have anxiety that drives them to perfectionism, but they may have real problems in school or extracurricular activities that they need help with. Assess for such problems by asking:

- Are the adolescent's peers very hard on him or her? Is the adolescent being teased, bullied, or embarrassed?
- Are there classroom demands for public performance?
- Do teachers, coaches, or other authority figures have expectations the adolescent fears he or she cannot meet?
- Is all of the adolescent's leisure time organized?

In these cases, anxiety management must include specific problem-solving for peer problems and extracurricular or classroom demands. That will help distinguish whether the anxiety remains once the anxiety-producing situations are resolved. In other words, you will be able to see whether the adolescent can relax after the environmental problem has been solved. If the anxiety persists, anxiety-disorder treatments will be necessary.

Elderly adults usually have the fewest demands for performance, but as people with TMA age, they may face problems managing anxiety when their activity is limited by health and mobility. Loss of activity can increase anxiety. Also be sure to check on:

- Health changes (e.g., a problem with vision or hearing that could be an obstacle to social engagement)
- Losses of friends
- Changes in residence

Devise a plan to reestablish activities that compensate for the changes.

S.I.M.P.L.E. PLAN TO CONTROL TMA

If you have TMA, chances are good that you will want to do everything at once. Remember there is no perfection, only progress! So select one of the methods outlined in this chapter and make a S.I.M.P.L.E. plan to start on it. For example, let's say you pick "life balance." Your S.I.M.P.L.E. plan might look something like Figure 11.4.

Now fill out your own S.I.M.P.L.E. plan.

S.I.M.P.L.E. Plan to Control TMA

Life Balance

S: What is the *symptom* or situation? *I am spending 12 hours a day on my commute and workday.*

I: What is the *impact* on my life? *I am not exercising at all and I am more sluggish and gaining some weight.*

M: What *method* am I trying? *I will increase the amount of time I spend walking each day by going out at lunch for a 30-minute walk. On weekends I will do at least one very brisk walk for 45 minutes.*

P: Practice plan. *I don't need to practice walking, but I will put gym shoes and socks in the backpack I take into work with me so I have the shoes there.*

L: Lifework. *Barring emergencies, I will walk every day during my lunch break after I've had something to eat.*

E: Evaluate. *I am going to tally my time walking on a card, and I will keep the card on the refrigerator so I can see the balance shift toward better self-care.*

Figure 11.4 S.I.M.P.L.E. Plan to Control TMA

S.I.M.P.L.E. Plan to Control TMA

Method: _____

S: What is the *symptom* or *situation?* _____
_____
_____

I: What is the *impact* on my life? _____
_____
_____

M: What *method* am I trying? _____
_____
_____

P: *Practice* plan. _____
_____
_____

L: *Lifework.* _____
_____
_____

E: *Evaluate.* _____
_____
_____

A FINAL WORD

People with TMA will always want to be active. The key to diminishing the negative effects of TMA is keeping balance in your life. You can discharge tension through positive activity and let go of the perfectionist behavior that keeps anxiety high. Your energy is going to help with this because you tend to do what you decide to do. Here's hoping you decide in the direction of balance and fun!

TWELVE

Technique #10:
Implement a Plan and Practice

This technique is about acquiring competence and confidence. The only way to achieve these is through life experience that expands or strengthens your knowledge and skills.

This chapter is intended to help people with panic and social anxiety (Chapter 11 was for people with generalized anxiety). It will show you how to develop competence and confidence in managing anxiety in work and social settings. Mastering this technique will require you to have worked on other techniques first in order to devise a plan and carry it out effectively. A big part of your confidence comes from knowing that even if you still get anxious from time to time, you will be able to manage it.

EDUCATE YOURSELF ON HOW THE BRAIN LEARNS AND UNLEARNS FEAR

You know, from experience, that your anxiety lessens when you avoid what you're afraid of. But your avoidance actually gives power to the situation you are avoiding. You may be thinking: *If I feel such relief by avoiding this situation, then it must* be *a dangerous situation, right?* Not right! Whether or not there was real danger, *your fear* was what made it seem dangerous.

There is just one basic principle you need to remember: You learned to be afraid by feeling afraid in a situation regardless of its actual risk. Your brain wants to make sure you stay out of scary situations—it wants to keep you safe. But the emotional part of your brain can't tell the difference between your fear of a genuine danger and the fear you generate because you *perceive* a situation as threatening. Thus, you can become afraid of being at a party, or in an elevator, or outside in a hurricane. Only one of those things is genuinely dangerous. But your brain will warn you away from all three if you have felt afraid in those situations.

If you want to unlearn fear, you have to be in the frightening situation without feeling afraid. *You have to be there without the scare!* Just as you can legitimately *learn* fear by being caught in a hurricane, you can also legitimately *unlearn* fear by successfully exposing yourself to the non-dangerous situations that scare you without succumbing to your fear.

Preparation is key here—you can't expect to quickly jump into real-life exposure. But with careful preparation, practice, and gradual exposure, you will be able to unlearn your fear. The methods in this chapter will help you do just that.

THREE DEEP BREATHS AND GOOD PREPARATION

When I was in high school, I was stricken with vicious stage fright, a form of performance anxiety, which is common for people with social anxiety. Waiting in the wings to go onstage, I would pray to God to make me fall over dead before I had to go out and sing. Dying may not have been the best choice of avoidance behaviors, but it was the only excuse the rest of the cast would accept if I missed my cue! My drama coach taught me one of the best anxiety management ideas I would ever learn. Intuitively creating diaphragmatic breathing because of her singing ability, she taught me to breathe slowly and deeply. She also taught me a cognitive framework for handling the anxiety, declaring, "All you need is three deep breaths and good preparation." Her "three deep breaths and good preparation" has become my model for getting rid of anxious behavior in any kind of anxiety-producing situation.

Hint: If you can calm yourself at will, you've got it made. Review Chapter 4 if you need more practice.

"Three deep breaths" stands for the ability to remain physically calm. It doesn't matter which breathing exercise you choose, or what kind of muscle relaxation you pair it with, as long as you use a physical calming technique when you face something that makes you anxious—ordering in a restaurant, speaking at a staff meeting, sitting in the middle of a theater, or driving on a toll road from which you can't exit for miles. Review Chapters 4 and 6 to refresh your memory on breathing and relaxation techniques. Also, listen to Track 10 on the CD, "5 Senses Centering Exercise," to help you stay cool and calm.

"Good preparation" stands for all the stages of getting ready to practice in real life. Having worked on your self-talk in Chapter 10 will be very useful for this. Changing your self-talk lays the groundwork for successfully using the methods discussed in this chapter.

IMPLEMENT A PLAN

Developing a solid plan involves getting motivated by setting goals, developing competence through skill-building, gaining confidence by practicing, and figuring out how to get real-life experience so that you can experience success. Take a look at Figure 12.1.

At the end of this section you'll have a chance to fill out your own plan to reduce anxiety. But first you need to learn the basics of setting goals, building skills, and practicing.

Set Goals

Why in the world would someone who wants to die rather than sing a solo in front of an audience go out to sing more than one time? Motivation! Once I got in front of the audience without dying, I enjoyed the act of singing. I had practiced it and I could do it well. I liked doing something I could do well. And then

Figure 12.1 Plan to Reduce Anxiety

The 10 Best-Ever Anxiety Management Techniques Workbook

there was the applause—it felt really good! With enough motivation, any person will face fear. And once you face your fear, it is diminished. I actually went on to major in speech and drama in college; learning that I could manage the fear and the motivation of loving the applause made that a desirable and doable choice.

Knowing what you stand to gain increases your motivation to face and overcome fear. It also helps you set goals. Setting goals solidifies motivation, because motivation is strengthened when you know that accomplishing your goal will make it easier to do next time.

What are *your* goals? Are they something like these?

- To place an order in a restaurant without breaking into a sweat
- To speak to my boss without a quivering voice
- To stay in class this semester
- To start interviewing for jobs

Make a list of your goals. They can be very general or specific.

What Are My Goals?

1. _____
2. _____
3. _____
4. _____
5. _____

No matter how specific or general you goals are, your next step is to see if you have the skills necessary to achieve them.

Identify the Skills You Need

For those who avoid social experiences because they are afraid of panic, there is a prerequisite to real-life exposure. If your social or work life is impeded by fear of panic—such as being unable to work on upper levels of a building because you may panic in an elevator, or being afraid of working in a large space because you may feel panic when you are far from an exit—then controlling panic attacks is your first order of business. See Chapters 1–4 for controlling the physiology of anxiety. Then, if you need them, the rest of these skills will need your attention.

Remember, *enjoying* doing something is not the same as being *able* to do it. For example, you may be able to smile, shake a stranger's hand, and say "it's nice to meet you" even if you don't particularly enjoy meeting new people. In other words, although you don't enjoy meeting new people, you *do* have the skills necessary to do it.

In identifying the skills you need, write down only the skills you actually *don't* have—do not include things you *can* do but don't *enjoy* doing.

The skills you will need depend on the kind of anxiety you have. Take a look at some of the following examples.

Social Skills

Check off each of the following items you *can't* do:

- ☐ Meet new people, introduce yourself, and ask questions of others
- ☐ Eat in public or eat with unfamiliar people at the table
- ☐ Speak in community meetings such as condo association or PTA
- ☐ Talk to teachers or administrative staff at your child's school
- ☐ Ask for a date or invite a new acquaintance to meet for coffee or lunch
- ☐ Other social skills: _____

_____

Personal-Business Skills

Check off each of the following items you *can't* do:

- ☐ Competently drive or use public transportation to get to work or social functions
- ☐ Run errands or shop for groceries or other necessities when stores are busy
- ☐ Be assertive enough to handle issues such as returning damaged goods or talking with customer-service representatives at banks or credit-card companies
- ☐ Ask questions of various services personnel about the cost of goods and services

---

The 10 Best-Ever Anxiety Management Techniques Workbook

- ☐ Sign checks or credit slips in front of a clerk
- ☐ Talk with retail personnel, asking questions about purchasing or exchanging goods
- ☐ Talk with medical personnel and clarify information about medical conditions and treatments
- ☐ Deal with insurance companies for claims and coverage concerns (medical, home, auto, etc.)
- ☐ Talk with ease to your child's coaches or tutors or make appointments and financial arrangements for lessons
- ☐ Other personal business skills: _____

_____

Work or Career Skills

Check off each of the following items you *can't* do:

- ☐ Ask questions of a supervisor about your work duties
- ☐ Ask for training on a job task that you cannot perform adequately
- ☐ Attend training sessions with or without colleagues present
- ☐ Independently obtain additional training by finding and attending certification or education programs available in the community
- ☐ Discuss schedule-change requests with a manager
- ☐ Talk socially with a coworker at break
- ☐ Talk with a coworker about a work situation
- ☐ Enter a meeting room and choose where to sit in unstructured settings; greet colleagues as they enter the room
- ☐ Interview for a job
- ☐ Do what is necessary to make presentations at your job
- ☐ Offer comments during a group/committee meeting
- ☐ Other work or career skills: _____

_____

If you checked more than two items in any of these lists, you will need some basic skill-building in that area to dispense with anxiety. (If you *do* have the necessary skills and simply are not using them because you are avoiding situations, go ahead and skip the skill-building section that follows.)

Build Skills

It's very important to be honest with yourself about what you need to learn—you'll never become truly confident unless you have the competence (skills) to back it up. Once you've identified the skills you need, finding outside help to build them is the next step.

Hint: See the Recommended Reading and Resources section for a list of skill-building workbooks.

There are many ways to learn skills. If you already have a therapist, consult him or her first. You can also consider using workbooks for social-skills and assertiveness training. Several are listed in the Recommended Reading and Resources section of this workbook. You can also learn skills in group therapy, which is very useful for those with social anxiety because you are learning with others.

Groups are often available for learning specific skill sets, such as assertiveness, social skills, conflict management, or anger management. You may have to hunt to find a local therapist who offers these kinds of groups, but often it's well worth the effort. Look at adult-education departments at community colleges for topics like public speaking, flirting, interviewing, etiquette, and Internet communication, as well as for one-time social opportunities (such as tours or theater performances) that give you a chance to be social with a focus for the conversation. These classes are often very inexpensive.

Practice Beforehand

This part of the plan is about gaining confidence. Many people resist practicing, even in private, because they are embarrassed. That is exactly why it is necessary. Not practicing before the real event is akin to memorizing a part in a play but never saying it aloud before going onstage for the first performance. Not even a completely relaxed actor would want to go on without a rehearsal.

The best way to approach practice is to first break down your goals into smaller, achievable steps.

Identify Achievable Steps

You have already identified your goals. Some of them may be specific; others may be broader. For the ones that are broader, you need to break the goal down into smaller steps to improve your chances at successfully achieving it.

For example, perhaps one of your goals was to learn to interview for jobs without looking nervous. This goal might be broken down into:

1. Be able to greet the people interviewing me
2. Be able to talk about myself
3. Be able to ask and answer questions without looking nervous

Go ahead and break your goal down into smaller steps.

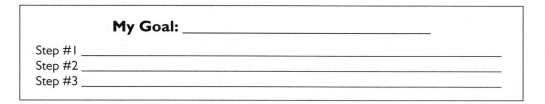

My Goal: _____

Step #1 _____
Step #2 _____
Step #3 _____

Now, break those steps down into even smaller steps. Figure 12.2 is an example of how you might do that.

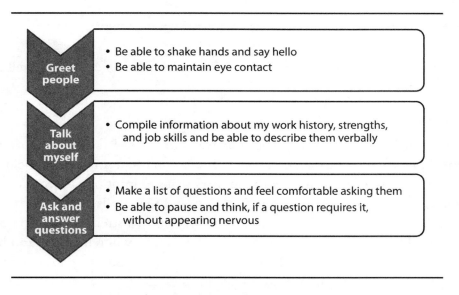

Greet people
- Be able to shake hands and say hello
- Be able to maintain eye contact

Talk about myself
- Compile information about my work history, strengths, and job skills and be able to describe them verbally

Ask and answer questions
- Make a list of questions and feel comfortable asking them
- Be able to pause and think, if a question requires it, without appearing nervous

Figure 12.2 Breaking Goals Down Into Achievable Steps

Identifying small steps that you can reasonably accomplish is the key to unlearning fear. Breaking off chunks too big for your temperament and skills is self-defeating. To assure success in unlearning fear, make sure you can do each step before going on to the next one. Use the following form to break your goals down into the smallest steps possible.

Now you're ready to begin practicing. It's best to find someone who will help you with this part of the plan.

Get a Helper

Who might be willing to help you practice your steps? It could be a parent, a therapist, a spouse or partner, or a friend. If you can't find someone to help you, be sure to at least speak your part out loud, perhaps in front of a mirror. Your lips will better remember what to do if they have said the words before.

When you practice, your brain gets a workout that strengthens it to do the real work. The more often you practice, the better you will remember. You literally form connections in your brain that will make it easier to remember what you have practiced when you are under pressure. The more you run through what you want to say or do, the less sensitive you will be, and anxiety symptoms will be less likely to appear.

Remember to Breathe During Practice

You're probably going to be nervous when you begin practicing, even though you know it's only a practice session. You may feel some shortness of breath or feel your heart start to pound. If this happens, just remind yourself that no one can see your heart beat and it will subside when you are done. You can diminish both heart rate and respiration by changing your breathing on purpose. Use diaphragmatic breathing, one-breath relaxation (see Chapter 6), or your favorite other breathing method to help you remain calm. It will also help you remember to breathe when you're in the real-life situation.

For example, suppose you are practicing speaking up at a staff meeting. To make the practice session as real as possible, you've decided to pretend that your dining room is the meeting room. You stand outside the dining room door and:

1. Feel yourself get tense as you imagine walking into the room.
2. Use one-breath relaxation as you walk through the door, and again as you take a seat at the table. (This calms you.)
3. Feel yourself get tense again as you anticipate having to speak.
4. Use one-breath relaxation again to stay physically calm until it is time for you to speak. (This allows your body to remain as quiet as possible so your symptoms will not be easily triggered.)
5. Actually speak up, loosely following the script you planned ahead of time.
6. Use one-breath relaxation to calm yourself again immediately after speaking.

Now, when you go into the actual meeting, you will better remember when and how to breathe.

Rate Your Anxiety Level During Each Practice Session

Again, when you first begin practicing, you're probably going to be pretty nervous. But the more you practice, the less nervous you'll become. Rating your anxiety level during each practice session is a way of being able to (1) visually see how your anxiety decreases, and (2) get a sense of when you're ready to stop practicing and begin the real thing.

This method worked particularly well for Darius. Darius was an extremely shy young man, but he was also a reliable employee at the retail store where he worked. He wanted to take an accounting class that met on Saturday mornings at the community college, but his shift included weekends, and he knew his co-workers wouldn't be eager to trade shifts with him. He had told his manager when he was hired that he would be willing to work Saturdays, so now he felt very nervous about asking for this change. He wrote down what he wanted to say: "I know I agreed to work weekends, and I am still willing to work afternoons on Saturday. However, I want to advance my career and this class is important to me. It only meets on Saturday morning. Will you please schedule me off Saturday mornings during this semester?"

He had only one shot to say this to the manager, so it was important that he get comfortable with his speech. He had a week to get ready, so he knew he'd better practice a couple of times each day. He decided to do most of the practice sessions without help from a friend, because he didn't want to "bore them," but he did agree to try it once with a friend for the practice session preceding the actual meeting.

Darius did not expect to be completely calm when he talked to his manager, but thought he could be "pretty calm"—maybe a 2. He wanted to be between 0 and 1 when he practiced with his friend. He used a graph like the one in Figure 12.3 to rate his anxiety during each of 14 practice sessions. As you can see, his anxiety level did indeed drop to a 1 by the thirteenth session, and stayed at 1 during the fourteenth session with his friend.

Use the blank graph that follows Figure 12.3 to chart your own level of anxiety over the course of 14 practice sessions.

Recap

Let's go over your anxiety-reduction plan one more time (Figure 12.4).

Of course, the specifics of each of these steps will depend on what kind of goal you have set. Take a look at the following example of a mother who wants to be able to take her kids to the movies without having a panic attack.

The 10 Best-Ever Anxiety Management Techniques Workbook

Figure 12.3 Level of Anxiety Over 14 Practice Sessions

Anxiety-Reduction Plan

1. Set goals
2. Identify the skills you need
3. Build skills
4. Practice beforehand
   - Identify achievable steps
   - Break down steps into even smaller steps
   - Get a helper
   - Remember to breathe
   - Rate your anxiety level during each practice session

Figure 12.4 Anxiety-Reduction Plan

Example Anxiety-Reduction Plan

What is my goal? *I want to go to the movies with my kids.*

Do I have the skills to do this? *Yes—I used to go to the movies before I started panicking in movie theaters.*

How will I build skills to do this? *I don't need skill-building in this case because going to the movies doesn't require anything I don't know how to do.*

My plan to practice beforehand:
- *I will go to a movie alone so I don't bother my kids if I blow it.*
- *I will get to the theater a few hours ahead of the show so I have time to buy tickets and look around. Then I'll run some errands before coming back for the movie.*
- *I'll get to the theater early so I can sit where I am comfortable. I'll breathe and relax.*
- *I will get up, walk out, and then return during the previews—a time when I know no one will be bothered by my practicing leaving and returning in the dark.*

Figure 12.5 Example Anxiety-Reduction Plan

The 10 Best-Ever Anxiety Management Techniques Workbook

- _If I get nervous I have my reminder to breathe panic away. If I feel I need to leave to calm down, I will reenter the theater and sit down again to show myself I can._
- _I will repeat the above experience to be sure I am confident before I take the kids._

What are my anxiety-level ratings? _The first time I tried this, my anxiety was so high that I didn't return to the theater again after buying tickets. The second time, I was able to follow through on the whole plan— my anxiety was high (an 8) but I managed to get through it. The third time, my anxiety started at a 5, but by the time the movie was over I'd almost forgotten that this was a practice session, and when I left the theater my anxiety was 0._

Figure 12.5 Continued

DESENSITIZATION OF TRAUMA

Practicing before beginning real-life exposure is a way of desensitizing yourself to the feared situation. The plan described in this chapter works very well for people whose anxiety is not rooted in earlier trauma. There *are* valuable desensitization techniques for people who have suffered trauma, but they require help from a therapist and can't be taught in a workbook. Some of these treatments include: systematic desensitization, EMDR, energy therapies, and biofeedback or neurofeedback (see the Recommended Reading and Resources section for information on how to find these therapies). These can be excellent choices to help with desensitizing, especially if you have a history of having been shamed, bullied, humiliated, or terrified. It is not easy to bounce back from such life experiences without additional help.

REAL-LIFE PRACTICE

Once you have identified what you want to do, developed skills, and rehearsed to get desensitized, it's time to get out into real life. Practicing in real life should be done in small steps that gradually increase the length of time you spend in the situation in order to allow you to leave while still feeling calm. This is how you will unlearn your fear.

Theater actors prepare for performances by going through several exposures of increasing intensity—a process that serves as a good metaphor for anxiety reduction. After rehearsing their lines in a practice room or other space, actors get on stage to know where to stand (that's like the desensitization stage of your plan). Then there is a technical rehearsal in which actors wear their costumes and the crew tests whether lights, music, curtains, and scene changes work smoothly. No one is in the audience, even though this is conducted just like the real thing. Then comes the dress rehearsal, usually with a small audience of people connected to the performers and some of the crew. In professional theater, there are low-cost "preview performances" while the little mistakes are ironed out. Your real-life practices are the equivalent of these rehearsals. Just like with the tech and dress rehearsals that few people will even see, be sure you start out with steps that have minor consequences for either success or failure. For example, if you fear driving on the highway, don't start by getting on the road during rush hour in a downpour.

The 10 Best-Ever Anxiety Management Techniques Workbook

The most difficult part of this technique is getting exactly the right degree of exposure to build competence without risk of diminishing confidence. Just like with the practice sessions, you will use a graph to rate your level of anxiety during each real-life exposure. If you see your anxiety level go down with each subsequent real-life practice session, you know you've achieved the right degree of exposure. If it begins an upward trend, you need to think about taking smaller steps. Use the graph on page 206 to rate your anxiety over 14 real-life practice sessions.

Figure 12.6 shows an example of setting up the real-life practice for a man with social anxiety who wants to be able to go to happy hour with his coworkers.

Real-Life Practice

What is my goal? *I want to go to happy hour on Friday with my coworkers.*

Do I have the skills to socialize? *I have practiced making small talk about work, the weather, and local sports teams. I think I am ready.*

My real-life practice sessions:
- *Stay first for 30 minutes.*
- *Then stay 60 minutes the next time, but without ordering food, so I won't worry about eating with them.*
- *Then I will order food, and stay until I have eaten at least some of it.*
- *After that, I will stay until the group breaks up for the evening.*

What are my anxiety-level ratings? *My anxiety stayed at about an 8 during the first real-life practice session. It was actually higher during the next session when everyone ordered food, but when I saw that no one even noticed that I wasn't eating with them, it went down to a 7. During the next session it was at a 6. It got a little higher when I ordered food, but went back down again after I'd eaten a couple of bites and then let the waitress clear the plate. In the last session it was at a 4, even while we all ate. I'm pretty sure it'll be even lower the next time.*

Figure 12.6 Real-Life Practice

Figure 12.7 Don't Sweat It!

Remember: It Won't Always Go Perfectly

What happens if you fail or get anxious while making a small step? Be grateful! This is a great opportunity to evaluate what kinds of things trip you up, and to review and adjust your plan so that you get better and better. Whatever you do, do not dwell on it or tell yourself bad things about yourself. Everyone makes mistakes. Have some reasonable expectations (Figure 12.7).

FROM IMPLEMENTING A PLAN TO REAL-LIFE PRACTICE: A RECAP

The idea behind this technique is that success paves the way for more success, even if there are a few bumps and setbacks along the way. This is how your brain unlearns fear—every time you are able to do something without getting panicky or embarrassed, the emotional part of your brain says, "Hey, wait! I thought that would be dangerous, but I guess I was wrong. Apparently I *don't* always have to send out a warning the next time I'm in that situation." And even if you *do* get panicked or embarrassed, seeing that you can live through it also helps calm the brain. The whole process—from implementing a plan to real-life practice—is shown in Figure 12.8.

Remember that you will keep building on your successes until the whole goal is met. At every stage the new learning (or unlearning of fear) lays groundwork for the next step to occur safely. It is not until the whole goal is met that the safe experience will completely turn off the warning signal for that specific situation in the future.

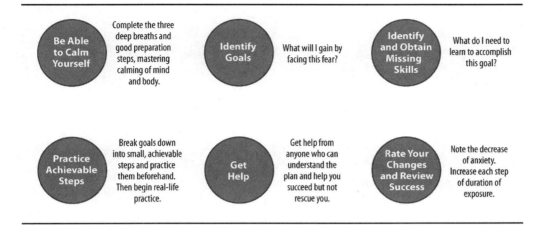

Figure 12.8 From Implementing a Plan to Real-Life Practice

A FINAL WORD

This is the one chapter that does not easily lend itself to a S.I.M.P.L.E. plan because of the number of steps that planning for exposure requires. That is why there is so much emphasis on planning small steps and evaluating their success. Preparing by implementing a plan and practicing are the keys to "being there without scare" and unlearning fear. Practice means exactly that: making trial runs to do things you have not been able to do before. And no one goes out on a practice run without preparation. If you are preparing for an athletic event, you learn skills, get advice about how to do those skills, try them out, see what works and what doesn't, and then try them out again before the competition. Your three deep breaths and preparation—setting goals, learning skills, and practicing—will get you ready to go out into real life. Practice makes possible.

Recommended Reading & Resources

This section contains suggestions for further reading and is divided by topic, in alphabetical order.

Children, Adolescents, and Anxiety

Chansky, T. (2004). *Freeing your child from anxiety.* New York: Broadway Books.

Foxman, P. (2004). *The worried child.* Alameda, CA: Hunter House.

Pincus, D., Ehrenreich, J., & Spiegel, D. (2008). *Riding the wave workbook.* New York: Oxford University Press.

Wagner, A. (2005). *Worried no more.* Rochester, NY: Lighthouse Press.

Nutrition and Supplements

Amen, D., & Routh, L. (2003). *Healing anxiety and depression.* New York: Putnam.

Brown, R., Gerbarg, P., & Muskin, P. (2009). *How to use herbs, nutrients & yoga in mental health care.* New York: Norton.

Des Maisons, K. (2008). *Potatoes, not Prozac.* New York: Simon & Schuster.

Hendler, S., & Rovik, M. S. (Eds.). (2001). *Physician's desk reference for nutritional supplements.* Des Moines, IA: Thompson Healthcare.

Weil, A., (2001). *Eating well for optimum health.* New York: Harper Paperbacks.

Relaxation, Meditation

Davis, M., Eschelman, E., & McKay, M. (2008). *The relaxation and stress reduction workbook.* Oakland, CA: New Harbinger.

Ensley, E. (2007). *Prayer that relieves stress and worry.* Forston, GA: Contemplative Press.

Hanh, T. N. (1975). *The miracle of mindfulness.* Boston: Beacon.

Newberg, A., & Waldman, M. R. (2009). *How God changes your brain.* New York: Norton.

Siegel, D. (2007). *The mindful brain: Reflection and attunement in the cultivation of well-being*. New York: Norton.

Sensitivity

Zeff, T., & Aron, E. (2004). *The highly sensitive person's survival guide: Essential skills for living well in an overstimulating world (step-by-step guides)*. Oakland, CA: New Harbinger.

Sleep and Exercise

Perlis, M. (2008). *The cognitive-behavioral therapy of insomnia*. New York: Springer.
Ratey, J. (2009). *Spark: The revolutionary new science of exercise and the brain*. New York: Little, Brown.

Social Skills

Brennan, I. (2011). *Anger antidotes*. New York: Norton.
Brenner, H. (2003). *I know I'm in there somewhere*. New York: Gotham Books.
Buckingham, M., & Clifton, D. (2001). *Now, discover your strengths*. New York: Free Press.
Carter, L., & Minirth, F. (1993). *The anger workbook*. Nashville, TN: Thomas Nelson.
Cooper, B. (2008). *Social success workbook for teens: Skill-building activities for teens with nonverbal learning disorder, Asperger's disorder, and other social-skill problems*. Oakland, CA: New Harbinger.
Khalsa, S. (1996). *Group exercise for enhancing social skills and self-esteem*. Sarasota, FL: Professional Resource Press.
Korb-Khalsa, K., Leutenberg, A., & Azok, S. (1992). *SEALS+PLUS: Self-Esteem and life skills: Reproducible activity-based handouts created for teachers and counselors [spiral-bound]*. Wilkes-Barre, PA: Wellness Reproductions and Publishing, Inc., available through Courage to Change.
Korb-Khalsa, K., Leutenberg, A., & Azok, S. (1998). *Life management skills III: Reproducible activity handouts created for facilitators [spiral-bound]*. Wilkes-Barre, PA: Wellness Reproductions and Publishing, Inc., available through Courage to Change.
Madson, P. R. (2005). *Improv wisdom*. New York: Crown.
Myles, B., Trautman, M., & Schelvan, R. (2004). *The hidden curriculum: Practical solutions for understanding unstated rules in social situations*. Overland Park, KS: Autism Asperger Publishing Company.
Nay, T. R. (2012). *Taking charge of anger*. New York: Guilford.
Novotni, M. (1999). *What does everybody else know that I don't know?* Plantation, FL: Specialty Press.
Robbins, J. M. (2002). *Acting techniques in everyday life*. New York: Marlowe.
Seigel, D., & Hartzell, M. (2003). *Parenting from the inside out*. New York: Putnam.
Wahlberg, T. (2011). *Finding the gray*. St Charles, IL: The Prairie Clinic.
Wilson, B., & DeMaria, R. (2009). *He's just no good for you: A guide to getting out of a destructive relationship*. Guilford, CT: GPP Life.

Therapy Methods

Ecker, B., & Hully, L. (2007). *Coherence therapy manual*. Available on their website www.dobt.com.

Eifert, G., McKay, M., & Forsyth, J. (2005). *Acceptance and commitment therapy for anxiety disorders*. Oakland, CA: New Harbinger.

McMullin, R. (2005). *Taking out your mental trash*. New York: Norton.

O'Hanlon, B. (1999). *Do one thing different*. New York: William Morrow.

Pincus, D., Ehrenreich, J., & Spiegel, D. (2008). *Riding the wave workbook*. New York: Oxford University Press.

Wehrenberg, M. (2008). *The 10 best-ever anxiety management techniques*. New York: Norton.

Wehrenberg, M. (2010). *The 10 best-ever depression management techniques*. New York: Norton.

Wehrenberg, M., & Prinz, S. (2007). *The anxious brain*. New York: Norton.

Non-Talk Therapy Methods

Childre, D., & Martin, H. (1999). *The Heartmath solution*. San Francisco: Harper Collins.

Demos, J. (2005). *Getting started with neurofeedback*. New York: Norton.

Gallo, F., & Vincenzi, H. (2000). *Energy tapping*. Oakland, CA: New Harbinger.

Pratt, G., & Lambrou, P. (2000). *Instant emotional healing*. New York: Random House.

Shapiro, F. (2001). *Eye movement desensitization and reprocessing: Basic principles, protocols, and procedures* (2nd ed.). New York: Guilford.

Women's Health Issues

Northrup, C. (2006). *The wisdom of menopause*. New York: Bantam.

Northrup, C. (2006). *Women's bodies, women's wisdom*. New York: Bantam.

Websites & Other Resources

For Help with Addictions

1. National Institute of Drug Addiction
   www.nida.nih.gov
2. National Clearinghouse on Drug and Alcohol Addiction
   1-800-729-6686
3. Addiction Self-Help:
   - www.alcoholics-anonymous.org
   - www.rational.org
   - www.smartrecovery.org
   - Cocaine Anonymous at www.ca.org
   - Education and guidance for sexual addiction at www.Candeohealthysexuality.com
   - Education and guidance for recovery from substance abuse at www.Candeosubstanceabuse.com
4. Family Help with Addiction:
   - www.al-anon.alateen.org
   - www.familiesanonymous.org

For Help with Anxiety

1. Anxiety Disorder Association of America: www.adaa.org
2. Coming soon: www.candeoanxietyanddepression.com

For Help with Attention Deficit Disorder

Among many good sites, start with www.CHADD.org

For Help with Irritable Bowel Syndrome

A helpful website for people with anxiety and IBS: http://www.webmd.com/ibs/guide/stress-anxiety-IBS.

For Help with Sleep

For ideas to sleep better, consult www.sleepeducation.com, sponsored by the American Academy of Sleep Medicine (www.aasmnet.org).

For Help with Trauma

1. Contact the International Society for Traumatic Stress Studies for resources, pamphlets, education for professionals and the general public. E-mail: istss@istss.org
2. Sidran Traumatic Stress Foundation www.sidran.org
3. International Critical Incident Stress Foundation: www.icisf.org

For Information on Herbal Medicine and Supplements

1. National Library of Medicine and the National Institutes of Health sponsor Medline, which has a variety of options for nutritional and alternative medicine treatments. Visit the website at: medlineplus.gov
2. The American Botanical Council. From their website: "At the American Botanical Council, we are passionate about helping people live healthier lives through the responsible use of herbs, medicinal plants. We are an independent, nonprofit research and education organization dedicated to providing accurate and reliable information for consumers, healthcare practitioners, researchers, educators, industry and the media." Visit the website at: abc.herbalgram.org

For Information and Help with Obtaining Medication

National Alliance on Mental Illness provides a list of resources for people who cannot afford medication or who do not have insurance. They also have information and resources for other mental illnesses.
1-800-950-NAMI (6264)
www.nami.org/Template.cfm?section=about_medications&Template=/ContentManagement/contentDisplay.cfm&ContentID=19169

For Information on Other Therapies

1. Learn more about EMDR and how to be trained or find a therapist who practices EMDR. From the website: "EMDR International Association (EMDRIA) is a professional association […] committed to assuring that therapists are knowledgeable and skilled in the methodology of EMDR […]. This website provides information and services to the greater EMDR community including clinicians, researchers, and the public that our members serve. (Scott Blech, CAE, Executive Director)

www.emdria.org
Email: info@emdria.org
2. Learn more about energy therapies
   • www.emofree.com
   • www.energypsych.com
   • www.instantemotionalhealing.com

Mental Health Organizations

1. Anxiety Disorder Association of America
   www.adaa.org
2. National Institute of Mental Health
   www.nimh.nih.gov
3. National Institute of Mental Health
   www.nimh.nih.gov
4. Obsessive-Compulsive Foundation
   www.ocfoundation.org
5. American Psychological Association
   www.apa.org
6. American Psychiatric Association
   www.psych.org

Index